AI Bubble: How to Survive the Next Stock Market Crash

A book of

Geoffrey Perrin de Monmouth & A.Auffray

Table of contents

Table of contents.. 1
Preface.. 4
    By Thomas Andrieu... 4
Foreword.. 6
    Disclaimer.. 8
Prologue... 9
Chapter 1. Introduction.. 11
    1.1 Presentation of the subject... 11
    1.2 Objectives of the book.. 12
    1.3 Why prepare for a stock market crash....................... 14
Chapter 2: Understanding Speculative Bubbles..................... 16
    2.1 Definition and history of financial bubbles.................. 16
    2.2 Case studies: Tulipomania, Internet Bubble, Subprimes........ 17
    2.3 Bubble formation mechanisms................................... 19
Chapter 3: The AI Economy... 22
    3.1 History and evolution of artificial intelligence............. 22
    3.2 The impact of AI on financial markets........................ 23
    3.3 Leading companies in the AI sector........................... 26
Chapter 4: Warning Signs of a Bubble................................... 29
    4.1 Economic and financial indicators.............................. 29
    4.2 Investor behavior.. 31
    4.3 Analysis of current trends in the AI sector.................. 33
    4.4 Expert opinions on the warning signs of a Bubble: Stéphane Deo, Bill Gates, Alan Greenspan.. 46
Chapter 5: Stock Market Crash Scenarios............................. 51
    5.1 How a bubble bursts... 51
    5.2 Possible scenarios for an AI crisis.............................. 52
    5.3 Comparison with previous crashes............................ 61
Chapter 6: Anticipation scenario for an AI-related crisis........ 67
    6.1 Economic and financial context................................. 67
    6.2 The Spark of Infatuation... 67
    6.3 The Heat of Illusion.. 68
    6.4 The Health Crisis: the "Helion Flu" Virus.................... 68

AI Bubble: How to Survive the Next Stock Market Crash

- 6.5 The Bursting of the Bubble..69
- 6.6 Repercussions...69
- 6.7 Epilogue: Reconstruction... 70
- **Chapter 7: Are we in a crash scenario in 2024, in real life?.. 71**
  - 7.1 Context and Economic Conditions since July 2024... 71
  - 7.2 The Nikkei Crash of August 5, 2024..73
- **Chapter 8: Consequences of a Stock Market Crash... 75**
  - 8.1 Overall economic impact... 75
  - 8.2 Effects on Technology Companies and Investors..77
  - 8.3 Consequences for the Real Economy...79
- **Chapter 9: Anticipating and Detecting a Crash.. 82**
  - 9.1 Strategies for Detecting an Impending Crash... 82
  - 9.2 Use of Financial and Economic Indicators... 84
  - 9.3 Comparison of Stock Market Overvaluations of the 7 Sublimes with a Reference Value..90
  - 9.4 Using the Hindenburg Omen..91
  - 9.5 The Importance of Strategic Monitoring.. 94
  - 9.6 Expert opinion: Analysis of past bubbles and anticipation of future bubbles............99
  - 9.7 What do the Kondratieff and Juglar cycles tell us? When might this AI bubble arrive?.. 100
- **Chapter 10: AI Bubble Preparedness Strategies...103**
  - 10.1 Diversification of Investments..103
  - 10.2 Use of Derivative Products and Options... 105
  - 10.3 Warrants and ETFs to consider to prevent a bubble.. 106
  - 10.4 Importance of Liquidity and Cash Reserves..108
  - 10.5 Tips for strengthening your portfolio during periods of growth.......................110
- **Chapter 11: Responding in Times of Crisis... 112**
  - 11.1 Sales and Loss Reduction Strategies.. 112
  - 11.2 How to seize opportunities in times of decline.. 114
  - 11.3 The Role of Psychology and Discipline in Crisis Management.......................... 116
  - 11.4 Techniques for securing your investments during a crash................................ 118
- **Chapter 12: Taking Advantage of Post-Crash Opportunities...121**
  - 12.1 How does the market recover after a crash?... 121
  - 12.2 Investment Opportunities After a Crisis... 122
  - 12.3 Strategies to bounce back and benefit from the recovery.................................124
- **Chapter 13: Nvidia and the AI Bubble.. 126**
  - 13.1 History and Performance of Nvidia...126
  - 13.2 What the media and analysts think about the spectacular growth and current valuation.. 128
  - 13.3 Risk analysis: overvaluation and volatility... 130
  - 13.4 Expert Opinions: Short Sellers and Bullish Investors..................................... 132

AI Bubble: How to Survive the Next Stock Market Crash

13.5 Possible scenarios for the future of Nvidia... 133
13.6 Lessons for investors (bubble or no bubble?).. 136

Chapter 14: Should we take refuge in Gold?... 139
14.1 Gold as a safe haven: History and outlook... 139
14.2 Performance of gold in times of crisis... 141
14.3 Advantages and disadvantages of investing in gold............................. 142
14.4 Comparison with other safe havens... 144
14.5 Expert Analysis: Gold Returns and Recession Protection................... 147
14.6 Gold Investment Strategies: Physical, ETF, Mining Stocks................. 149
14.7 Gold Investor Testimonials... 150

Chapter 15: Should we take refuge in real estate?.................................. 153
15.1 Analysis of the current real estate market.. 153
15.2 Risks and opportunities in real estate in 2024..................................... 155
15.3 Signs of a real estate bubble.. 157
15.4 Impact of high interest rates and regulations...................................... 159
15.5 Comparison with other asset classes... 161
15.6 Expert opinions on the future of real estate.. 163
15.7 Real estate investment strategies during volatile times...................... 165

Chapter 16: Divergent opinions: Correction or New Bubble?................. 170
16.1 Analysis of the current correction of technology stocks..................... 170
16.2 Arguments Against the Existence of an AI Speculative Bubble and a Near Crisis.... 172
16.3 Growth Prospects for Technology Companies..................................... 173
16.4 Arguments from Wedbush analysts on the durability of the correction............... 176
16.5 Growth Predictions for Tech Stocks.. 178
16.6 An Extended View of Stock Market Capitalization Forecasts: The Technological Titans at the Dawn of a New Era............... 181
16.7 Strategies for Taking Advantage of Correction................................... 183
16.8 Economic Analysis and Lessons from the Film The Big Short............ 186

Chapter 17: Current Economic Weaknesses that would make the Stock Market Crash more serious than before... 189
17.1 Detailed Analysis of Current Economic Weaknesses and Risks of Stock Market Crash............ 189

17.2 The Situation in France: Ability to Survive a Stock Market Crash............ 192
17.3 Inevitability of Corrections: The Threat of Cycles................................ 194
17.4 The 6th Wave of Innovation: A New Technological Era in Perspective............... 196

Conclusion: Innovation Cycles and Bubbles, an Inevitable Balance of the Economy 199
Annexes... 201

AI Bubble: How to Survive the Next Stock Market Crash

Preface

By Thomas Andrieu

While reading the considerable work of Geoffrey Perrin de Monmouth and Aymeric Auffray, the story of Isaac Newton suddenly came to mind. As John Maynard Keynes described it in 1942, Newton was "the last great mind who looked at the visible and intellectual world with the same eyes that began building our legacy nearly 10,000 years ago." »

Isaac Newton is best known for his groundbreaking discoveries in physics, but he also had a second life as an economist and speculator. After spending years in Cambridge unraveling the secrets of nature, in 1696 he became director of the Royal Mint. Its new mission was to guarantee the stability of the currency by adjusting the weight of gold and silver coins and fighting counterfeiting.

However, Newton was not as accurate in economics as he was in physics. In 1720, he was swept up in the speculative frenzy surrounding the South Sea Company. Founded in 1711 to manage part of the British public debt in exchange for exclusive trading rights in South America, this company aroused immense enthusiasm, and the value of its shares climbed dizzyingly.

Initially cautious, Newton invested in early 1720, making a profit of around £7,000. But giving in to the general euphoria, he reinvested when prices were at their highest. In September 1720, the bubble burst after a nearly 10-fold increase in prices, causing stocks to fall sharply to historic lows. Newton lost around £20,000, a colossal sum for the time, far more than his annual salary of £500-600 at the Royal Mint.

This story teaches us two lessons. First, that financial bubbles are a constant in the economy and that they will continue to appear. Then, this story shows us that the most brilliant minds can succumb to collective frenzies. Legend has it that Newton said: "I can calculate the movement of celestial bodies, but not the madness of men".

AI Bubble: How to Survive the Next Stock Market Crash

Remember that the vast theater of our society, with its details and intrigues, reveals a prodigious phenomenon of cyclical dynamics. A study of stock market statistics over the last 150 years shows that financial panics sometimes occur every two decades. But when excess money creation or debt comes into play, stock market valuations can move dangerously away from economic reality.

Despite the pathological regulations, the bubbles continue to follow one another. A major innovation is often at the origin of these more or less important bubbles: in 1720, it was trade with the Americas; today, it is artificial intelligence. Bubbles are not irrational in the long run, because innovations do eventually diffuse, but excessive speculation is often too impatient to respect the natural rhythm of the economy.

This book is a call to slow reason that only a multi-centenarian investor could have. In the stock market as elsewhere, it is always better to be cautious than too inclined to follow the ephemeral fashions of the times. Because above fashions, economic cycles are established.

Thomas Andrieu
(August 2024)

Foreword

It may seem at least incongruous, if not downright preposterous, to talk about a financial bubble and its inevitable crash while artificial intelligence is in full triumphant rise, driven by gargantuan investments. However, some economists, in their infinite wisdom or their insatiable thirst for pessimism, are beginning to frantically wave the red flag. Some are already claiming that this wave of frantic investments is nothing other than a bubble ready to burst.

As a trader, myself, embarked on this ship of technological opportunities called the "sublime 7" and other gems of AI, I felt the irrepressible need to put on my analyst glasses. My goal? Understand, anticipate, and perhaps even sense the warning signs of a potential correction, or even a financial catastrophe. Certainly, I do not have the arrogance to compare myself to the oracles of the markets, to eminent economists and analysts. Nevertheless, I will try to remain understandable to you, the individual traders, who participate in this AI revolution with all the optimism of those who still think that the future will be bright.

Rest assured, I will not hesitate to direct you to works and analyzes more complete than mine when it is appropriate for you to benefit from the work of people more knowledgeable than me on the various levers impacting the economy.

Now, to cut short any suspense as useless as it is thrilling about my conclusions: yes, my dear friends, I think in view of the various signals and previous crises that a bubble is indeed forming, and it could not choose worse moment. With a global economy already under pressure, stuck between fragile liquidity, starving savings rates and titanic state debts, all in a geopolitical context that borders on fire, the specter of a bubble bursting is enough to give rise to cold sweats. However, the wild optimist that I am can't help but think that, despite everything, we still have some great climbs to come. So, let's take advantage of these last

AI Bubble: How to Survive the Next Stock Market Crash

waves before the tide goes out and we are all left high and dry and also prepare for the likely trend reversal by the end of 2025.

Certainly, the mini crash of the Nikkei in August 2024 gave us a taste of what could await us, but we are assured that the American economy is doing wonderfully, thank you very much. Not to mention, of course, the traditional disruptions that the next American elections promise us – a classic of the genre, regulars will say.

In summary, we are faced with crystal clear indicators: the bubble seems to be there. But, my friends, don't panic, it's urgent not to worry. It's up to you to draw your own conclusions with all these elements and prepare yourself as best as possible for a future which promises to be as tumultuous as it is fascinating. In short, life, what.

AI Bubble: How to Survive the Next Stock Market Crash

Disclaimer

My dear readers, before plunging into the stock market abyss where figures and percentages happily frolic, I must therefore remind you, not without a touch of solemnity, that this modest work in no way claims to guide you towards the golden shores of the assured fortune. No, far be it from me to have the absurd idea of turning into a market guru, handing out investment advice on the fly that is as enlightened as it is infallible.

So know this, my friends: what you will read here is only the humble opinion of a trader who, just like you, struggles to understand the unfathomable and the unpredictable. It's up to everyone to form their own opinion, in complete autonomy and with that little glimmer of critical thinking which, I hope, has not completely abandoned you.

As for these famous past performances, allow me to tell you with all due seriousness: they in no way predict future performances. It's not me who says it, it's the Financial Markets Authority, and, between us, it doesn't tend to joke about this kind of thing. In short, keep in mind that the future, like humor, is often unpredictable... and that the biggest falls sometimes come after the greatest flights.

AI Bubble: How to Survive the Next Stock Market Crash

Prologue

If you've opened this book, it's probably because you're looking to understand something, maybe even find some meaning in this mess we call the financial market. Maybe that's what pushed me to write this book too: a quest to grasp what's really happening.t when markets boom and bust.

The world of financial markets, with its bubbles and crashes, is not much different from the stories we tell to cope with the complexities of life. It is a complex, often confusing story, where the protagonists are not heroes but investors, speculators, and sometimes, victims of a system that seems out of control.

In the pages that follow, we will explore stories of speculative follies and economic disasters. We will talk about Tulipomania, this period when the Dutch lost their minds over flowers, a fable which, as incredible as it is, is very real. Then there was the South Sea Bubble, a financial adventure that turned into tragedy, and of course, the Dotcom Bubble of the 90s, where everyone thought you could just stick a ".com" on it. at the end of a name to become a millionaire.

And here we are, at the dawn of a new era, that of artificial intelligence. A technology that promises to change everything, but which could also be the next big bubble. It's fascinating and terrifying at the same time. Are we ready for what is to come? I'm not sure, but I know that understanding the past is a good start.

This book is not just a lesson in economics. It is an exploration of human behavior in the face of uncertainty and the promise of wealth. It's a journey through time, a look at mistakes and triumphs, hopes and disillusionments. In a way, it's an attempt to make some sense out of all this chaos.

So, get ready to dive into the stories of bubbles and crashes. Discover the ups and downs of the global economy. Maybe you'll find some

AI Bubble: How to Survive the Next Stock Market Crash

answers, or maybe just more questions. But one thing is certain, you will never look at financial markets the same way again.

Welcome to "AI Bubble: How to Survive the Next Stock Market Crash". Take your time, read carefully, and above all, think. Because in the end, that's all we can really do.

AI Bubble: How to Survive the Next Stock Market Crash

Chapter 1. Introduction

So many mysteries, so many passions, so many dramas play out every day in this world of financial markets, where numbers dance and fortunes are made and unmade in the blink of an eye. Entering the world of financial bubbles means venturing into a fascinating labyrinth where history, economics, and human psychology intersect and intertwine in an often unpredictable ballet.

In this book, we will try to unravel the secrets of these bubbles which, like the wildest dreams, form, burst and leave in their wake a trail of disillusionment and hard-won wisdom. Financial bubbles are not just economic phenomena; they are reflections of the human soul, with its excesses, its hopes and its fears. And, by understanding them, perhaps we can learn to better navigate this complex and capricious world.

1.1 Presentation of the subject

Financial bubbles, these ephemeral creations of our markets, are comparable to works of baroque art: flamboyant, spectacular, but often fragile and ephemeral. A financial bubble forms when asset prices rise exponentially, often due to rampant speculation and a collective belief in endless gains.

To illustrate this complex dance, it is essential to return to the first historical examples. The Tulipomania of the 1630s in the Netherlands is a perfect example. Tulips, then rare and precious, saw their value rise to absurd levels. Bulbs were exchanged for entire houses until, inevitably, the bubble burst, destroying the dreams and savings of many speculators.

Closer to us, the South Sea Bubble at the beginning of the 18th century demonstrates the same human folly. Promises of fabulous riches overseas pushed South Sea Company stock prices to dizzying heights, before reality overtook the dreams, leading to a precipitous fall and a major economic crisis in England.

And how can we not mention the Internet bubble of the 1990s? At the dawn of the digital age, investors flocked to the stocks of technology startups, convinced that every company with a ".com" was a gold mine. Valuations rose astronomically, before collapsing abruptly in 2000, leaving behind a landscape of devastation but also rich in lessons.

This chapter aims to explore these phenomena in depth, to decipher the underlying mechanisms that lead to the formation of bubbles and to learn from past mistakes. Understanding financial bubbles means understanding a fundamental aspect of our economic history, and perhaps becoming wiser and more prudent in our own financial adventures.

Bubbles, like dreams, are beautiful and dangerous. They remind us of the fragility of our certainties and the power of our illusions. By studying them, we hope not only to understand the errors of the past but also to prepare for a more serene and enlightened future.

1.2 Objectives of the book

Let's speak frankly. If you are reading this book, it is because somewhere you are looking for answers, maybe even comfort. The world of financial markets can seem as impenetrable and confusing as a Kafkaesque novel. Financial bubbles, with their fleeting burst and abrupt collapse, are like those strange dreams that leave a lingering impression, long after waking up. In this context, the objectives of this book are simple, but essential.

1.2.1 Understand to no longer be surprised

The first ambition of this book is to help you understand. Understand how and why these bubbles form. Understand the mechanisms that fuel them and the warning signs of their bursting. It is often said that those who ignore history are doomed to repeat it. By delving into the stories of past bubbles, we hope you can avoid falling into the same traps.

1.2.2 Anticipate to better prepare

Once you have this understanding, the next step is anticipation. Financial markets are never static. They evolve, fluctuate and sometimes behave completely irrationally. This book aims to give you the tools to anticipate changes, to read between the lines of financial reports, to spot the subtle clues of a bubble in the making.

1.2.3 Protect what matters

Then there is protection. Investing is much more than seeking to maximize profits. It is also, and perhaps above all, protecting what we have. Whether it's your savings, your investments or your peace of mind, this book will teach you how to implement diversification and risk management strategies to protect yourself from the vagaries of the markets.

1.2.4 Seize hidden opportunities

Finally, there are the opportunities. Crises, as painful as they are, are often times of great opportunity. For those who know where to look, the rubble of a burst bubble can hide treasure. We'll show you how to identify these opportunities, how to act with caution and discernment, and how to take advantage of turbulent times to build something strong and lasting.

In short, this book is not just a practical guide. It's a sort of survival manual for modern times. A faithful companion that we hope will help you navigate the often murky waters of the financial markets with a little more confidence and a lot more wisdom. Because at the end of the day, all we really want is to no longer be caught off guard, to no longer be helpless spectators to our own mistakes. And if this book can give you that, then it will have served its purpose.

1.3 Why prepare for a stock market crash

Let's face it, preparing for a stock market crash is a bit like keeping an umbrella in your bag on a sunny day. You hope you never need it, but you know the sky could get dark at any moment. And when it starts to rain heavily, you'll be glad you planned ahead.

Stock market crashes are not urban legends or stories to scare children. They're real, and they strike without warning, often when you least expect it. Why prepare for a stock market crash? Because history has shown us, again and again, that markets are fickle and can descend into chaos in the blink of an eye.

Look back, and you'll see a litany of stock market crashes that all followed similar patterns: a rapid rise, fueled by euphoria and speculation, followed by a precipitous fall. From the Tulipmania of the 17th century to the subprime crisis of 2008, bubbles burst, markets plunged, and investors were left picking up the pieces. Preparing for a crash means taking note of these lessons from the past and refusing to be taken by surprise.

In the world of financial markets, uncertainty is the only constant. Values go up and down, often for no apparent reason. New technologies, political changes, health crises – everything can influence markets. By preparing for a crash, you accept this uncertainty and steel yourself against it. You can't predict the next crash, but you can make sure you're prepared for it.

Investing is not just about making your money grow. It's also about protecting what we already have. A stock market crash can wipe out years of gains in an instant. By diversifying your investments, maintaining sufficient liquidity and establishing risk management strategies, you protect your assets against market ups and downs. You build walls around your garden, so it can withstand storms.

Stock market crashes, as devastating as they are, are also times of opportunity. For those who are ready, market declines can provide unique buying opportunities. Stocks that were overvalued can become affordable, neglected sectors can recover. Preparing for a crash also means being ready to seize these opportunities, to invest intelligently when others panic.

Finally, preparing for a stock market crash means giving yourself peace of mind. Knowing you've taken steps to protect your investments lets you sleep soundly, even when the economic news is bleak. It's knowing that, no matter what, you have done everything in your power to protect yourself and thrive.

In short, preparing for a stock market crash is an act of wisdom and foresight. It's about accepting the reality of financial markets and ensuring that when the storm hits, you're not only standing tall, but ready to move forward. Because at the end of the day, all we can really do is be ready.

Chapter 2: Understanding Speculative Bubbles

Speculative bubbles, you see, are these fascinating and frightening things at the same time. They rise and rise, like a balloon that you inflate with excitement mixed with fear, because you know full well that it will eventually burst. Human nature, in all its glory and madness, is at the heart of these phenomena. The financial markets are only the theater where this strange and repetitive play is played out.

When we talk about speculative bubbles, we are talking about this collective excitement that pushes people to invest irrationally, convinced that prices will rise indefinitely. And then, inevitably, reality hits, the balloon pops, and dreams of wealth turn into nightmares of loss.

2.1 Definition and history of financial bubbles

Let us first try to put words to this elusive phenomenon. A financial bubble is like that strange feeling you get when you are convinced that something extraordinary is going to happen, and everyone around you shares this belief. It is the collective euphoria that pushes people to buy assets at unreasonable prices, in the hope of selling them for even more.

Let's take a historical example to illustrate all this: the South Sea Bubble, in the 18th century. The South Sea Company promised incredible riches through trade with South America. The company's shares soared to dizzying heights, buoyed by exaggerated promises and frenzied speculation. In 1720, reality set in again, and the bubble burst, leading to a major financial crisis in England. Another lesson from history that we have seemed to forget time and time again.

The 19th century had its own share of madness with the Railway Bubble. The railways represented the future, a promising industrial revolution. Investors speculated massively, fueled by unrealistic expectations of future profits. When these expectations were not realized, the bubble burst, and the railway dream turned into an economic nightmare.

These stories, as varied as they are, share a common thread: irrational exuberance, the belief that prices will continue to rise endlessly, and the inevitable return to reality. Understanding these bubbles means understanding human nature a little better, with its strengths and weaknesses. It's about preparing yourself not to repeat the mistakes of the past, or at least to try. Because at the end of the day, what we're all looking for is to avoid finding ourselves picking up the pieces when the dream turns into a nightmare.

2.2 Case studies: Tulipomania, Internet Bubble, Subprimes

Let's look now details some of history's most famous bubbles, moments when human greed reached such absurd heights that their bursting was as dramatic as it was predictable. Tulipomania, the Internet Bubble and the Subprime crisis are textbook cases which show how the excesses of speculation can lead to economic disasters.

Where did we come from (1637)

Let us return to Tulipomania, this almost mythical tale from the 17th century, where tulip bulbs became more precious than houses. In the Netherlands in the 1630s, the fascination with tulips took a frenzied turn. Bulbs, especially those with rare colors and patterns, were traded at exorbitant prices. People sold their most valuable possessions to invest in these flowers. It was a period of pure speculative madness.

Future contracts, a concept that was ahead of its time, allowed people to buy bulbs they didn't even own yet. In 1636, a single bulb could sell for up to 10,000 guilders, the equivalent of the annual income of a prosperous artisan or the price of a beautiful house on the canals of Amsterdam. And then, in February 1637, the bubble burst. Prices collapsed almost overnight, sometimes falling to 1/100th of their peak value, leaving thousands financially devastated. What began as a simple passion for flowers ended up revealing the dangers of unbridled speculation.

AI Bubble: How to Survive the Next Stock Market Crash

The Internet Bubble (2000)

Let's move forward a few centuries to the end of the 1990s, a time when the Internet was becoming the new El Dorado. Everyone wanted a piece of this new digital world, and investors rushed to buy stock in any company that had a ".com" at the end of its name. Valuations have reached stratospheric levels, often without the slightest economic basis. Startups without a viable business model have seen their shares rise to dizzying heights.

Take the example of Pets.com, an emblematic company of this period. Launched in 1998, its stock reached a peak of $11 in February 2000, only to collapse to less than $1 in November of that year, leading to the company's bankruptcy. Another notable casualty was Webvan, an online grocery delivery company, which raised nearly $400 million in its 1999 IPO, only to see its stock fall from $34 to less than $1 in 2001, leading to its closure.

The Subprime Crisis (2008)

Finally, let's talk about the Subprime crisis of 2008, an episode that is still fresh in our memories. In the United States, banks began making mortgage loans to high-risk borrowers, encouraged by rising house prices and the illusion that those prices would continue to rise indefinitely. These loans were often restructured and sold as complex financial securities to other investors.

The most emblematic case of this crisis is undoubtedly that of Lehman Brothers. In 2007, Lehman Brothers stock reached nearly $86. When the bubble burst, real estate values plunged, borrowers defaulted, and the securities backed by those mortgages collapsed. Lehman Brothers declared bankruptcy in September 2008, causing its stock to fall to $0.

Bear Stearns, another major financial institution, also succumbed, going from a stock priced over $170 in 2007 to being acquired by JPMorgan Chase for just $2 per share in March 2008, although that price was later raised to $10 per share.

Conclusion

These three case studies show how destructive financial bubbles can be. They reveal the excesses of speculation and the dangers of human greed. But they also offer crucial lessons. By understanding these historical events, we can better prepare ourselves and avoid repeating past mistakes. Because, at the end of the day, what we're all looking for is to navigate this uncertain world with a little more wisdom and caution.

2.3 Bubble formation mechanisms

LFinancial bubbles are fascinating and disconcerting phenomena that capture the imagination of investors and economists, and yet always collapse with a bang, leaving a wake of ruin and disillusionment in their wake. Understanding the mechanisms of bubble formation is like trying to grasp the mist at daybreak: elusive, but so essential to avoid getting lost in the twists and turns of human greed.

The breath of collective euphoria

It all starts with a wave of enthusiasm, that initial flame that ignites minds and gives rise to crazy hopes. Whether it's a technological innovation, a major discovery or simply a passing fad, something triggers the enthusiasm of the crowds. The first investors, visionary or lucky, see their bets rewarded, thus attracting other followers. Collective euphoria then takes hold of the markets, and prices begin to rise, slowly at first, then exponentially.

The illusion of infinite growth

At the heart of bubble formation lies the illusion of infinite growth. Investors are beginning to believe that prices can only continue to rise. This belief, fueled by stories of dazzling success and quick wins, spreads like wildfire. Reason gives way to irrational exuberance, to borrow the words of former Fed Chairman Alan Greenspan. The media, analysts, and even governments often participate in this fervor, extolling the merits of the assets in question.

Speculation and leverage

As prices rise, investors become more and more daring. Speculation is in full swing. Buyers no longer care about the intrinsic value of assets; they only think about reselling them at a higher price. Leverage, this practice of borrowing money to invest more, amplifies the phenomenon. The gains are multiplied, but so are the potential losses. Banks and financial institutions, swept up in the wave, facilitate these practices by offering credit on increasingly lax conditions.

Red flags ignored

Meanwhile, voices are being raised to warn of the dangers of this frenzy. But in the whirlwind of euphoria, these warnings are often ignored or ridiculed. The warning signs of an impending crisis – blatant overvaluations, excessive debt, the disconnect between prices and economic fundamentals – are being swept under the rug by a majority convinced that "this time it's different".

The inevitable breakup

Finally, like an over-inflated balloon, the bubble bursts. A spark is often enough to trigger the collapse: bad economic news, a change in monetary policy, or simply the collective realization that prices are unsustainable. Panic then grips the markets. Investors attempt to sell en masse, precipitating a fall in prices. Banks are tightening their credit, bankruptcies are increasing, and the economy is entering recession.

Lessons to be learned

AI Bubble: How to Survive the Next Stock Market Crash

Every bubble that bursts leaves us with valuable lessons. They remind us that caution is required, that greed and fear are two sides of the same coin, and that history, although often ignored, invariably repeats itself. By understanding the mechanisms of bubble formation, we can hope to better navigate the turbulent waters of financial markets, armed with the wisdom that only experience, even indirect experience, can offer us.

Thus, by diving into the twists and turns of these financial phenomena, remember that each bubble, each burst, is only a reflection of our hopes and our excesses, a constant reminder of the fragility of human constructions in the face of unpredictable reality.

Chapter 3: The AI Economy

Artificial intelligence. Just saying these words almost feels a chill in the air, a mixture of wonder and fear. It's like conjuring up a kind of modern magic, an invisible power that already shapes our world in a thousand ways, often without us realizing it. If you are here, reading this book, it is because somewhere, you also feel this piqued curiosity, this desire to understand how this mysterious AI infiltrates the corners of our economy.

This chapter is an invitation to discover the mysteries of artificial intelligence, to untangle the threads of its history and to grasp the colossal challenges that it carries within it. The AI economy is not just about numbers and technology; it is a human saga, made of dreams, battles and silent revolutions.

3.1 History and evolution of artificial intelligence

The story of artificial intelligence is a bit like an old legend, full of unexpected twists and colorful characters. To understand where we are today, we need to go back to before AI became a buzzword.

It all begins in the 1950s, a time when scientists were just beginning to scratch the surface of what machines could accomplish. Alan Turing, this somewhat tormented genius, laid the first stone with his famous Turing test, wondering if a machine could think. Imagine this: a man sitting in front of a machine, trying to see if it could hold a conversation that would be indistinguishable from that of a human. It was like a challenge to the future.

Then there was John McCarthy, who coined the term "artificial intelligence" in 1956 at the Dartmouth conference. This gathering marked the official start of AI research, with ambitions that seemed almost naive at the time: to create machines capable of doing everything a human mind can do. Little did they know how long and winding the road would be.

The following decades were a mix of dazzling progress and periods of disillusionment. The 1960s and 1970s saw advances in the understanding of natural languages and strategy games, but also major obstacles. The computers of the time simply weren't powerful enough to realize the dreams of these pioneers. We often talk about "AI winters", those periods when enthusiasm and funding dried up, leaving researchers to work in the shadows, like modern alchemists persevering against all odds.

It was not until the 1980s and 1990s that AI emerged from its long slumber. The appearance of expert systems, capable of simulating human reasoning in specific domains, has given new hope. But it was truly at the dawn of the 21st century that AI began to show its full potential. Advances in computing power, the rise of the Internet and the massive availability of data have allowed AI to take off.

Today, artificial intelligence is everywhere. She races cars, recommends songs, diagnoses illnesses, and even writes articles. Neural networks and deep learning have opened up perspectives that were unimaginable just a few years ago. But with these advances also come ethical questions, fears and hopes, like shadows that dance in the light of this new dawn.

The story of AI is one of perseverance, grandiose visions and unrelenting realities. It is a human story, deeply human, where each step forward is marked by the courage and madness of those who dare to dream of a different future. And in this future, we are all actors, whether we like it or not, each trying to understand, to tame, and perhaps even to master this intelligence which promises to redefine our world.

3.2 The impact of AI on financial markets

The impact of artificial intelligence (AI) on financial markets is both profound and broad, promising to transform many industries and unlock never-before-seen investment opportunities. By integrating AI into their processes, businesses can not only improve productivity, but also develop new products and services that better meet consumer needs.

AI Bubble: How to Survive the Next Stock Market Crash

Improved productivity and new opportunities

According to a PwC study, AI could add up to $15.7 trillion to the global economy by 2030. Much of this increase will come from productivity gains. For example, companies using AI tools to automate complex and repetitive tasks can redirect their human resources towards higher value-added activities. This concerns various sectors, ranging from health to finance, including manufacturing and professional services.

Examples of companies integrating AI to increase their turnover

Morgan Stanley has identified several categories of companies that will particularly benefit from AI:

1. **Margin Expanders** : These companies are using AI to reduce their operational costs. For example, a tax services company is using AI to process a much larger number of tax returns without increasing its headcount.
2. **Trailblazers** : Those who develop new products or services based on AI. One notable example is an online food delivery service that uses AI to improve customer service and increase average order sizes.
3. **Price Raisers** : Companies adding AI-based features to justify price increases. A video conferencing company has introduced an AI assistant that summarizes missed meetings, adding significant value for its users.
4. **Input Suppliers** : Suppliers of the core technologies needed for AI, such as semiconductor manufacturers. With the growing demand for computing capacity for AI, companies like Nvidia and Intel are well positioned to take advantage of this trend.

Future outlook and vigilance

Investments in AI offer long-term growth prospects, but they are not without risks. It is crucial for investors to remain selective and pay attention to valuations to avoid speculative bubbles.

AI Bubble: How to Survive the Next Stock Market Crash

The impact of artificial intelligence (AI) on financial markets has become a central topic for investors and analysts. In 2024, this technology continues to reshape the financial landscape, not only by optimizing companies' internal processes, but above all by creating massive and sometimes speculative investment opportunities.

The rise of technology companies thanks to AI

Tech companies investing heavily in AI have seen their valuations soar. For example, Nvidia, a major player in manufacturing GPUs used for AI applications, reported 176% year-over-year stock growth in 2024. This impressive rise is driven by the growing demand for gaming power. calculation needed for AI models. Nvidia, with a market capitalization exceeding $1 trillion, is an emblematic example of this investment frenzy (Investopedia).

Impact on Nasdaq and financial markets

The Nasdaq, an index composed mainly of technology companies, benefited from this wave of optimism around AI. In 2024, the Nasdaq saw growth of 30%, largely driven by AI-related companies. This growth has been fueled by investors betting on the future potential of AI, often with no direct relationship to these companies' current revenues. This creates a situation where valuations can appear disproportionate to actual economic fundamentals (World Economic Forum) (BlackRock).

Examples of businesses benefiting from AI

1. **Microsoft** : Microsoft has integrated AI into its Azure and Microsoft 365 services, with tools like Copilot based on GPT models developed by OpenAI. By 2024, 65% of Fortune 500 companies were using these services, increasing the productivity and efficiency of their operations (Investopedia).

2. **Amazon** : Amazon uses AI to improve the customer experience with Alexa, optimize internal processes through AWS, and offer AI services to other companies. These initiatives have helped keep Amazon at the forefront of technological innovation and market growth (Investopedia).
3. **Adobe** : Adobe has integrated AI capabilities into its products for digital marketing, content creation and document management. Although its recent stock performance has been less spectacular than that of some other AI giants, the company remains well positioned to benefit from the growing adoption of AI across various industries (Investopedia).

A speculative bet?

The current craze for stocks of technology companies investing in AI is reminiscent of the dotcom bubble of the 2000s. High valuations are often based on expectations of future growth rather than current performance. This speculation raises questions about the sustainability of these price increases. Investors should be aware of the risks inherent in this situation and consider diversified strategies to protect themselves against a possible market correction (J.P. Morgan | Official Website).

In conclusion, AI offers significant investment opportunities and has a major impact on financial markets. However, this investment frenzy also carries risks, and a balanced and informed approach is essential to navigating this rapidly changing landscape.

3.3 Leading companies in the AI sector

Artificial intelligence (AI) is redefining the global economic landscape, and a few key companies, nicknamed the "Sublime 7", dominate this sector. These companies concentrate much of the investment in AI, attracting both massive speculation and hopes of significant future gains.

AI Bubble: How to Survive the Next Stock Market Crash

The "sublime 7" of AI

1. **Nvidia (NVDA)** : Nvidia is a key player thanks to its GPUs, essential for training AI models. In June 2024, Nvidia saw its market capitalization exceed $3 trillion, even briefly reaching the top position among global market capitalizations. However, this valuation was short-lived, and the stock experienced some volatility thereafter.
2. **Microsoft (MSFT)** : Microsoft continues to integrate AI into its Azure and Microsoft 365 services. With tools like Copilot, the company has seen massive adoption by Fortune 500 companies. In 2024, Microsoft also saw a significant increase in revenue related to AI, thus strengthening its position in the market.
3. **Alphabet (GOOGL)** : Google's parent company is investing heavily in AI through its Google Cloud AI and DeepMind initiatives. In 2024, Alphabet saw notable revenue growth driven by these technologies, solidifying its position among AI leaders.
4. **Amazon (AMZN)** : With AWS and Alexa, Amazon uses AI to improve its services and optimize its internal processes. Integrating AI into its logistics operations has enabled Amazon to maintain its leading position in the e-commerce market.
5. **Meta Platforms (META)** : Meta is investing in AI to improve its recommendation algorithms and virtual reality products. In 2024, Meta launched several new AI-based features, which led to growth in its advertising revenue.
6. **Tesla (TSLA)** : Tesla uses AI to develop its autonomous vehicles. The company continues to improve its autonomous driving capabilities, attracting massive investments and seeing an increase in its stock value.
7. **Apple (AAPL)** : Apple, initially late in the AI race, caught up by announcing "Apple Intelligence" at WWDC 2024. This announcement caused its stock to climb 7.3% in one day, reaching an all-time high of $207.15 (Investopedia) (InvestorPlace).

Stock market performance in 2024

In 2024, the announcements of first quarter results caused spectacular increases for these companies. Nvidia, for example, grew 10% in a single day after announcing results that beat analysts' expectations. However, as of July 2024, several of these companies, including Apple and Nvidia, have suffered significant declines in their stock values, despite strong financial results. This volatility illustrates the speculative nature of AI investing, where future expectations play a crucial role in current stock valuations.

In short, although the AI "Sublime 7s" show enormous potential and captivate investor interest, it is essential to recognize the risks of overvaluation and speculation in this area. Investors must remain vigilant and well-informed to navigate this ever-changing landscape (Investopedia) (InvestorPlace) (InvestorPlace).

Chapter 4: Warning Signs of a Bubble

You know, financial bubbles are a bit like those strange dreams you sometimes have, where everything seems perfectly logical until you jolt awake, your heart pounding, and realize something is wrong. not. Bubbles form in a mixture of collective euphoria and denial, and they always end up bursting, often when you least expect it. But how can we see these bubbles coming? How can you feel the stirring beneath the surface before everything collapses?

The warning signs are often there, within reach, for those who know how to look. This chapter is dedicated to these indicators, those subtle but telling clues that can alert us to an impending bubble.

4.1 Economic and financial indicators

There are days when everything seems to be going well, when the markets go up and up, and every investment seems like a genius decision. But behind this façade, there are signs, discreet but persistent clues that something is wrong. Economic and financial indicators are our first tools to detect a bubble in formation.

Excessive Growth in Asset Prices

A classic first sign is excessive growth in asset prices. When you see stocks, real estate or commodities reaching dizzying heights in a very short period of time, it's time to ask yourself questions. This rapid growth is often fueled by speculation rather than solid fundamentals. Take the example of dot-coms in the 90s: valuations exploded without there being any real profits to justify them.

Price/Earnings Ratio (P/E) Abnormally High

Another key indicator is companies' price-to-earnings (P/E) ratio. When this ratio becomes abnormally high, it means that investors are paying very high prices compared to the companies' real profits. A high P/E may be justified by expected future growth, but when it becomes pervasive and disproportionate, it is often a sign of market overvaluation. For example, before the subprime bubble burst in 2008, the P/Es of financial companies were exorbitant compared to their actual performance.

Interest Rates and Easy Credit

Interest rates play a crucial role in the formation of financial bubbles. When interest rates are low, borrowing money becomes less expensive, which incentivizes consumers and businesses to take more risks. Easy access to credit fuels demand for assets, driving up prices. This situation creates an illusion of prosperity and encourages speculative behavior.

However, when central banks raise interest rates to curb inflation or cool an overheated economy, the cost of borrowing increases. This can quickly reverse the trend, as borrowers find it harder to repay their debts, and demand for assets falls. This dynamic can precipitate the bursting of a bubble. For example, before the subprime crisis, historically low interest rates fostered an explosion of risky mortgage lending, which led to a massive housing bubble.

Debt and Easy Credit

The ease with which consumers and businesses can obtain credit is also an important indicator. A period of easy credit fuels speculation as it becomes too easy to finance asset purchases with borrowed money. When debt levels climb and credit is distributed indiscriminately, it creates instability that can precede a crisis. This was the case with subprime mortgages in the United States before the 2008 crisis.

Collective Euphoria and Sheep Behavior

Finally, collective euphoria is perhaps the most difficult indicator to quantify but the most obvious to observe. When everyone around you is talking about investing in a certain type of asset, when the media is filled with success stories and even the taxi driver is giving you stock tips, it's time to be wary. Herd behavior pushes prices to unsustainable levels, as we saw with Tulipomania or more recently with cryptocurrencies.

In summary, to see a bubble coming, you have to be attentive, almost like a detective, always on the lookout for the warning signs. Economic and financial indicators do not lie, they are the silent messengers of a coming storm. And in this world where rationality often gives way to euphoria, knowing how to read these signs can mean the difference between a devastating loss and a cautious exit.

4.2 Investor behavior

Understanding investor behavior during financial bubbles is crucial to anticipate and potentially avoid significant losses. Investment decisions are often influenced by cognitive biases and emotions, which can lead to irrational behavior and unpredictable market cycles.

Irrational exuberance and herd behavior

One of the most prominent characteristics of financial bubbles is irrational exuberance, where investors become excessively optimistic. They begin to massively buy assets, driven by the illusion that prices will continue to rise indefinitely. This behavior is often fueled by the herding behavior, where individuals follow the actions of others without doing any real personal analysis. For example, during the dot-com bubble of the late 1990s, investors bought shares of tech startups without a viable business model simply because "everyone else was doing it" (Money Investors).

Psychological Bias

Psychological biases play a central role in investment decisions. Here are some of the most common:

- **Overconfidence** : Investors overestimate their abilities to predict market movements or choose the right stocks, which pushes them to take excessive risks. This overconfidence can lead to excessive trading and substantial losses when the market turns (Wall Street Oasis).
- **Loss aversion** : Investors feel the pain of losses more intensely than the pleasure of gains. This may lead them to hold on to losing investments for too long, hoping that they will recover, rather than cutting their losses in time (Gapodox).
- **Confirmation bias** : Investors seek information that confirms their pre-existing beliefs and ignore information that contradicts them. This reinforces biased decisions and can worsen the effects of bubbles (Money Investors) (Gapodox).

Sheepling Behavior and Financial Bubbles

Herding behavior, where investors follow the actions of the majority, is particularly evident during bubbles. For example, during the housing bubble before the 2008 subprime crisis, many investors purchased real estate at overvalued prices, believing that prices would continue to rise indefinitely. When the bubble burst, these same investors panicked and sold en masse, exacerbating the price drop (Jetir).

Strategies for Managing Behavioral Bias

To mitigate the impact of behavioral biases, investors can adopt several strategies:

- **Diversification** : Spread investments across different asset classes to reduce overall risk.

- **Strategic asset allocation** : Maintain an asset allocation based on financial goals and risk tolerance, rebalancing regularly to avoid impulsive decisions.
- **Education and Training** : Understand the fundamentals of investing and recognize cognitive biases to make more informed decisions.
- **Long term perspective** : Focus on long-term financial goals rather than short-term market fluctuations.
- **Professional Guidance** : Work with financial advisors to navigate market complexities and avoid emotion-based decisions (Wall Street Oasis).

In short, investor behavior during financial bubbles is often irrational and dictated by psychological biases. Understanding these behaviors can help predict the formation and bursting phases of bubbles, allowing investors to better prepare and make more rational decisions.

4.3 Analysis of current trends in the AI sector

4.3.1 Growth of AI investments

The year 2024 has seen a significant increase in investment in artificial intelligence (AI), both by large companies and startups. This push is driven by the promise of productivity gains, innovative new applications and the potential to transform industries. However, if they do not prove themselves, these massive investments could also be the warning signs of a speculative bubble.

Investments by large companies

In 2024, several tech giants have stepped up their investments in AI, often against a backdrop of high stock valuations reminiscent of past speculative periods:

- **Alphabet (Google)** : Alphabet has invested heavily in the development of its language models like Bard and Gemini.

Gemini, launched in December 2023, has been improved to outperform OpenAI's GPT-4. These advancements propelled Google shares nearly 60% in 2023, and this momentum continued in 2024 with the launch of Gemini Ultra, a model for highly complex tasks (Supermicro) (Investing.com).

- **Meta Platforms (Facebook)** : Meta continues to invest in AI to improve its recommendation algorithms and virtual reality products. In 2024, Meta launched several new AI-powered features, which led to growth in its advertising revenue (Supermicro).
- **Super Micro Computer (Supermicro)** : Supermicro has become a key player in AI infrastructure, with its high-performance servers optimized for AI applications. In 2024, Supermicro shares jumped 585% over the previous year, even outpacing Nvidia's performance. The company reported revenue of $3.85 billion for the third quarter of fiscal 2024, up 200% from the previous year. This growth is primarily driven by strong demand for its AI GPU platforms in the enterprise and cloud service provider markets (markets.businessinsider.com) (Supermicro).

Boom des startups IA

Startups also play a crucial role in the development of AI. In 2023, investments in AI startups reached $27 billion, with significant participation from tech giants. For example, Anthropic, backed by Amazon with an investment of up to $4 billion, is developing advanced AI models to rival those of Microsoft and Google (markets.businessinsider.com).

Attractive sectors and motivations

The most attractive sectors for AI investments include healthcare, finance, and manufacturing. Let's look at some real-world examples and their impact in 2024.

AI Bubble: How to Survive the Next Stock Market Crash

Health

AI is radically transforming the healthcare industry. For example, Hippocratic AI, a company specializing in large language models for health, raised $50 million in seed funding. Genesis Therapeutics, a drug discovery platform using generative AI, has closed a $200 million Series B round. Philips, in partnership with Amazon Web Services, is developing AI tools to improve medical image processing and optimize radiology workflows, enabling more accurate and faster diagnoses.

Finance

In the financial sector, AI is powering fraud detection, algorithmic trading, and personalized banking services. For example, JPMorgan Chase uses AI to analyze millions of transactions to detect potentially fraudulent anomalies, which has significantly reduced losses. Additionally, AI makes it possible to create personalized investment portfolios, offering advice based on individual customer behaviors.

Fabrication

AI is also revolutionizing manufacturing by automating processes and increasing efficiency. For example, General Electric uses AI systems for predictive maintenance of its industrial equipment, reducing downtime and maintenance costs. Additionally, Siemens is integrating AI technologies into its factories to optimize production lines and improve product quality.

In summary, increased investment in AI in 2024 is driven by the hope of profound transformation and significant improvement in productivity and innovation. Large companies and startups are at the forefront of this technological revolution, attracting billions of dollars in capital and promising to redefine the boundaries of what is possible with AI.

However, these investments have not yet shown real profits and also show signs of excessive speculation. High valuations and euphoria around AI technologies could indicate the formation of a bubble, similar to previous episodes of market overvaluation. Investors should remain vigilant and aware of the potential risks associated with this investment frenzy.

4.3.2 Innovative applications of AI

In 2024, artificial intelligence (AI) continues to revolutionize various sectors, including finance, logistics and consumerism. These innovations not only optimize operations, but also open up new possibilities for businesses. Let's explore some concrete, quantified examples of companies using AI to improve their products and services.

Finance

In the financial sector, AI is used to improve customer service, fraud detection, and risk management. For example, CitiBank uses Feedzai solutions to analyze millions of transactions and detect fraudulent activity, helping secure billions of dollars in daily transactions (Imaginovation). BlackRock, one of the largest asset management companies, uses AI to optimize its investment portfolios, increasing returns for its clients (Imaginovation). Robo-advisory platforms like Wealthfront and Betterment use AI algorithms to automate portfolio management, offering personalized wealth management services at a lower cost (Imaginovation).

Logistics

AI is also transforming the logistics industry by improving inventory management, supply chain planning and delivery. For example, Portcast provides real-time updates on shipping containers, allowing shippers to accurately predict cargo arrival times and reduce shipping costs (DataRoot Labs). Shippeo provides real-time visibility into multimodal transportation, helping logistics service providers manage shipments more efficiently and minimize disruption (Markovate). Uptake uses AI-powered maintenance analytics to assess the health of vehicle fleets, helping to reduce maintenance costs and increase driver mileage (Markovate).

Consumption

In the consumer sector, AI is used to personalize customer experiences and optimize operations. For example, consumer packaged goods giants like L'Oréal and Procter & Gamble use advanced data analytics to understand customer preferences and adapt their marketing strategies accordingly (BCG Global). Companies like PepsiCo are using AI to optimize their supply chains and manage inventory more efficiently, reducing costs and improving customer satisfaction (BCG Global).

Innovative applications of AI in 2024 show enormous potential to transform various sectors. However, the current exuberance and massive investments could also indicate speculative behavior, reminiscent of the warning signs of past financial bubbles. So bubble or no bubble?

Impact on financial markets

Despite all these very promising elements, the visible benefits on the financial markets are not always immediate. For example, despite significant investments in AI, L'Oréal's share price declined in June 2024. This decline could indicate that the market is skeptical about the short-term benefits of AI technologies, or that there is a growing disillusionment with high valuations based on future promises rather than current results. In other words, investors are starting to wonder whether the anticipated benefits of AI will actually materialize, which could be a harbinger of a speculative bubble (BCG Global).

4.3.3 Adoption of AI by businesses

The adoption of artificial intelligence (AI) by traditional businesses presents unique challenges and significant benefits. While some regions of the world are embracing the technology with enthusiasm, in Europe, AI adoption is occurring more slowly, in part due to lingering skepticism and regulatory concerns.

AI Bubble: How to Survive the Next Stock Market Crash

Challenges of AI adoption in Europe

In Europe, companies are often more cautious when it comes to integrating AI into their operations. According to a Deloitte study, European leaders show less interest in generative AI compared to their American and Asian counterparts. Nearly 20% of European respondents believe their industry pays too little attention to AI, reflecting cultural skepticism and concerns about associated risks, such as bias and privacy (Deloitte United States).

This caution is accentuated by a complex regulatory environment. The European Union's new AI Act, due to come into force in 2024, imposes strict requirements for high-risk AI systems, including fundamental rights impact assessments and transparency obligations. These regulations aim to ensure responsible use of AI, but they can also slow the adoption of the technology (Deloitte United States).

Benefits of AI adoption

Despite these challenges, companies that successfully integrate AI enjoy many benefits. IBM found that companies that overcame initial barriers invested more and reaped significant benefits from AI. Common AI use cases include IT process automation, security threat detection, and business analytics. These applications enable cost reductions, greater operational efficiency and improved customer satisfaction (IBM Newsroom).

AI Adoption Examples

1. **Finance** : HSBC also uses AI to improve regulatory compliance and detect fraud. Their AI system analyzes millions of transactions in real time, helping to spot suspicious behavior and reduce fraud losses.
2. **Logistics** : DHL has integrated AI to optimize its supply chains and delivery operations. AI helps predict package volumes, optimize routes and manage inventory, resulting in significant cost savings and improved logistics efficiency (Appian).
3. **Consumption** : Carrefour uses AI to personalize its customers' shopping experience. Using AI algorithms, Carrefour can analyze

purchasing behavior and recommend suitable products, thereby increasing sales and customer satisfaction (Appian).

In conclusion, although AI adoption in Europe is slower due to various challenges, companies that successfully integrate this technology see significant improvements in productivity and competitiveness. However, continued skepticism and strict regulations indicate that AI has not yet reached its full potential in this region, and companies must navigate carefully to balance innovation and regulatory compliance.

4.3.4 Regulations and ethics of AI

The rise of artificial intelligence (AI) has led to growing concerns about its responsible use. In response, new regulations are emerging across the world, and ethical questions are becoming central to the debate on AI. This section examines the efforts of governments and organizations to regulate AI and ensure its ethical use, while analyzing how these regulations could impact the warning signs of a bubble.

Emerging regulations

In 2024, the European Union finalized the AI Act, the world's first comprehensive AI law. This regulation imposes strict requirements for AI systems considered high risk, including impact assessments on fundamental rights and transparency obligations. The aim is to ensure that AI is used safely and fairly, but these requirements may also slow down innovation and the adoption of AI by European businesses (Skadden, Arps, Slate, Meagher & Flom LLP).

In the United States, the Securities and Exchange Commission (SEC) has proposed rules to address conflicts of interest posed by the use of AI by broker-dealers and investment advisors. In California, the California Privacy Protection Agency (CPPA) has introduced regulations for automated decision-making technologies under the California Consumer Privacy Act (CCPA). These rules aim to protect consumers from biased or non-transparent decisions made by AI systems (Skadden, Arps, Slate, Meagher & Flom LLP).

Ethical issues

The use of AI raises many ethical questions, particularly regarding privacy, algorithmic bias and liability. For example, AI models used for automated decision-making can perpetuate or even exacerbate existing biases if the training data is biased. Data privacy is also a major concern, especially when personal information is used to train AI models.

International bodies, such as the UN, have formed advisory groups to create global agreements on the governance of AI systems. In 2024, the Bletchley Declaration was signed by representatives from the EU, US, UK, China and 25 other countries, highlighting the importance of trustworthy AI and recognizing the potential dangers of general-purpose AI models (KPMG).

Impact on warning signs of a bubble

Regulations and ethical concerns can have a dual effect on warning signs of an AI bubble. On the one hand, strict regulations can slow the rapid adoption of AI, thereby mitigating some of the speculative excesses that fuel financial bubbles. On the other hand, regulatory requirements may increase costs and development times for AI technologies, which could deter investors in the short term.

However, if regulations are seen as a guarantee of safety and reliability, they could also strengthen investor confidence and encourage more stable and long-term investments. Ultimately, the balance between innovation and regulation will be crucial in determining whether the AI sector enters a phase of sustainable growth or risks seeing a new speculative bubble emerge (KPMG) (EY Assets).

4.3.5 Political impact on AI

Trade policies and political stances play a crucial role in the development of the artificial intelligence (AI) sector. In 2024, presidential candidate Donald Trump's statements and policies have particularly highlighted the issues of semiconductor taxation and restrictions on China.

AI Bubble: How to Survive the Next Stock Market Crash

Trump's positions on semiconductors and China

Donald Trump has announced his intention to impose tariffs of 60% on imports from China, aiming to accelerate the strategic decoupling between the two countries. He argues that these measures are necessary to protect the economic and national security of the United States, by promoting domestic production and limiting dependence on China.

Trump also proposed measures to tighten restrictions on the sale of critical technologies, such as advanced semiconductors, to China, in order to stunt the latter's technological progress.

Impact on the AI sector

These policies have significant implications for the AI industry, particularly for semiconductor companies like Nvidia and ASML. In July 2024, Nvidia shares fell 5% following the announcement of potential new restrictions on semiconductor technology exports to China. The decline reflects investor concern about the impact of these policies on the future earnings of the company, which generates about 22% of its revenue in China.

ASML, a Dutch company specializing in semiconductor manufacturing equipment, also saw its shares fall following the announcements. The prospect of increased restrictions overshadowed the company's strong results, which had reported a 24% increase in net bookings in the second quarter of 2024.

Potential implications for warning signs of a bubble

Political uncertainties and trade tensions can strongly influence financial markets. Protectionist policies and high tariffs can cause stock prices of technology companies to fluctuate, due to investor nervousness about the stability of supply chains and long-term growth prospects. Trump's announcements have shown that even well-established companies like Nvidia and ASML are not immune to the negative effects of these policies, which could indicate warning signs of a bubble in the tech sector if valuations are not supported by solid fundamentals.

In conclusion, Trump's policy stances on semiconductors and China in 2024 have major implications for the AI sector. They create a climate of uncertainty that can influence the warning signs of a bubble, highlighting the importance of increased vigilance on the part of investors and regulators to avoid speculative excesses in this critical area.

4.3.6 Impact of AI on the labor market

The impact of artificial intelligence (AI) on the job market is a complex and multifaceted topic. AI is not only transforming existing sectors but also creating new ones, thereby changing the skills required and the nature of jobs. Let's analyze the effects of AI on different sectors, the new jobs created, and the skills needed in this new economy.

Most affected sectors

Some sectors are more exposed to the impact of AI than others. According to PwC, the information technology (IT) and finance sectors have the highest proportion of tasks that can be automated. In IT, for example, tasks like software quality assurance and customer support are particularly affected. In finance, AI is used for tasks like bookkeeping, accounting and auditing, reducing the need for manual labor in these areas (PwC) (McKinsey & Company).

The health sector is also strongly impacted. McKinsey predicts a significant increase in demand for healthcare professionals and wellness technicians, due to the increasing implementation of AI in diagnostics and patient care (McKinsey & Company). The McKinsey report indicates that AI could transform work activities for many professionals, increasing demand for advanced technical skills in healthcare.

New jobs created

AI doesn't just replace existing jobs; it also creates new ones. For example, the number of "Head of AI" positions has increased by almost 14% since the end of 2022, and job postings mentioning "ChatGPT" and "GPT" have increased 21 times over the same period. These positions require specialized skills in machine learning, natural language processing, and AI development (HubSpot Blog).

The professional services, financial services, and manufacturing sectors also show strong demand for AI skills. The skills employers seek are changing at a 25% higher rate in occupations most exposed to AI, showing the growing importance of continuing education and acquiring new skills (PwC) (Visual Capitalist).

Skills required in the new economy

To stay relevant in a rapidly changing job market, workers need to learn new skills. AI and big data skills have become priorities for companies with more than 50,000 employees. Workers must be proficient in using AI to improve business performance, which includes skills in deep learning, predictive modeling, and data analysis (HubSpot Blog).

Training and professional retraining initiatives

Faced with these transformations, several training and professional retraining initiatives have emerged. For example, continuing education and reskilling programs are offered by online educational platforms like Coursera and Udacity, which offer specialized courses in AI and machine learning. Governments and businesses are also investing in training programs to help workers acquire the skills needed for the jobs of tomorrow (PwC) (McKinsey & Company).

AI Integration by Adecco

Adecco, a global leader in human resources services, has integrated AI into its recruitment processes to improve efficiency and accuracy. Tools like resume builders, chatbots to answer candidate questions, and automated resume reviews save time and optimize candidate selection. Adecco is also working on a career platform in collaboration with Microsoft to better match candidate skills to employer needs (Home | Adecco Switzerland) (Home | Adecco Switzerland).

In conclusion, AI is profoundly transforming the labor market, creating new opportunities while replacing some traditional tasks. Businesses and workers must adapt to this new reality by investing in continuing education and acquiring advanced skills to remain competitive in an increasingly automated economy. However, these rapid changes may also signal warning signs of a bubble, as exuberance around AI technologies could lead to overvaluations and unrealistic expectations regarding the immediate benefits of AI.

4.3.7 Long-term growth prospects

Artificial intelligence (AI) is poised to transform various industries, and its long-term growth prospects are promising. Let's explore the growth forecasts for the AI sector, anticipated trends, areas of potential growth, and the challenges ahead to maintain this momentum.

Growth Forecasts

According to a Goldman Sachs report, global investments in AI could reach $200 billion by 2025, fueled by increased demand in sectors like healthcare, finance and information technology. AI is expected to add around 7% to global GDP by 2030, equivalent to around $13 trillion (markets.businessinsider.com) (Fidelity Investments).

Anticipated trends

1. **Increased automation** : AI will continue to automate repetitive and complex tasks, increasing operational efficiency across various industries. For example, the use of robots and machine learning algorithms in manufacturing production lines is expected to become more widespread.
2. **Personalizing the customer experience** : Companies will increasingly use AI to analyze customer data and personalize services. This is already visible in the retail sector, where giants like Amazon are using AI to recommend products and optimize supply chains (InvestorPlace) (Schwab).
3. **Development of new medical applications** : AI will play a key role in personalized medicine, advanced diagnostics and drug

development. Companies like IBM Watson Health and Google Health are investing heavily in these areas to revolutionize healthcare.

Areas of Potential Growth

- **Health** : AI enables significant advances in disease diagnosis, electronic medical records management and the development of personalized treatments. Companies like NVIDIA and Intel are investing in AI platforms for medical research and healthcare (InvestorPlace).
- **Advertisement** : For example, Google uses AI to improve its search and advertising services, generating significant advertising revenue that funds more AI research and development (InvestorPlace)
- **Education** : AI can transform education by personalizing learning for each student, automating administrative tasks, and providing predictive analytics to improve educational outcomes. Startups like Coursera and Udacity are already integrating AI into their online learning platforms (Fidelity Investments).

Semiconductor Growth

The growth of semiconductors is a key factor for the expansion of AI. According to IDC, the semiconductor market is expected to grow 20% in 2024, mainly due to increasing demand for AI chips and the recovery of supply chains from the disruptions of 2023 (IDC). Industry giants like TSMC, Samsung, and Intel are investing heavily in new production capacities and advanced technologies to meet this growing demand (Uptrends.ai | Track Trending Stocks).

Challenges to overcome

1. **Ethics and regulation** : Ethical issues, such as algorithmic bias, data privacy and transparency, must be addressed to ensure responsible use of AI. Regulators must also find a balance between innovation and consumer protection (Fidelity Investments) (Schwab).

2. **Training and skills** : The transition to an AI-driven economy requires a skilled workforce. Businesses and governments must invest in training and reskilling to prepare workers for the jobs of tomorrow (InvestorPlace).
3. **Infrastructure and investment** : AI development requires robust technology infrastructure and continued investment in research and development. Businesses must collaborate with governments and academic institutions to maintain an environment conducive to innovation (markets.businessinsider.com).

In conclusion, the long-term growth outlook for the AI sector is extremely promising, with forecasts indicating a significant increase in adoption and investment. However, to fully realize this potential, it is essential to overcome ethical, training and infrastructure challenges. Businesses and governments must work together to create an enabling framework for innovation and ensure that the benefits of AI are shared equitably.

4.4 Expert opinions on the warning signs of a Bubble: Stéphane Deo, Bill Gates, Alan Greenspan

Identifying the warning signs of a financial bubble is a complex task that requires the analysis of a variety of economic and behavioral factors. To provide a more in-depth perspective, this chapter looks at the opinions of recognized experts in the economic and technological fields. Stéphane Deo, renowned economist, Bill Gates, technology pioneer, and Alan Greenspan, former chairman of the United States Federal Reserve, each bring a unique perspective on current and future dynamics of financial markets, particularly as they relate to AI and its potential impacts on bubble formation.

4.4.1 Stéphane Deo: Analysis of market prospects and associated risks according to Stéphane Deo, renowned economist

Stéphane Deo, renowned economist and head of market strategy at Ostrum Asset Management, is known for his in-depth analyzes of financial markets. According to Deo, warning signs of a financial bubble are often linked to fundamental imbalances in the economy, combined with irrational investor exuberance.

Deo points out that AI, while offering immense opportunities, could also lead to excessive valuations if investor expectations become outsized relative to economic realities. He warns against the tendency of markets to overvalue technology companies based on expectations of future growth without sufficient support from current fundamentals (Deloitte United States) (EVERYTHING).

One of Deo's main concerns is the increasing leverage used by companies and investors to finance their AI positions. High debt, coupled with inflated valuations, can create fertile ground for a bubble. It recommends a cautious approach, emphasizing the importance of portfolio diversification and risk management to mitigate the potential impacts of a market correction.

Deo also discussed the impact of monetary policies on financial markets. With historically low interest rates, there is an abundance of liquidity available, which can fuel speculative bubbles. However, normalizing monetary policies could quickly reverse this dynamic, increasing borrowing costs and reducing liquidity, which could precipitate a market correction.

In conclusion, Stéphane Deo calls for increased vigilance and rigorous evaluation of investments in AI technologies, taking into account not only the growth potential, but also the risks inherent in excessive valuations and excessive use of leverage.

4.4.2 Bill Gates: Bill Gates' perspectives on the future of AI, its economic and societal impacts, and precautions to take to avoid a bubble

Bill Gates, Microsoft co-founder and technology visionary, offers a unique perspective on the future of AI and its implications for the economy and society. Gates is optimistic about the potential of AI to transform key sectors like healthcare, education and agriculture. He sees AI as a powerful tool to solve some of humanity's most pressing problems, such as infectious diseases and world hunger.

However, Gates also warns of the risks of rushed and unregulated adoption of AI. He points out that the overvaluation of technology companies, fueled by excessive speculation, could lead to a financial bubble similar to that of dot-coms. Gates recommends several precautions to avoid this scenario:

1. **Regulation and ethics** : Gates emphasizes the importance of regulating AI to ensure it is used ethically and responsibly. It calls for clear standards to avoid algorithmic bias and protect data privacy.
2. **Investment in training** : For AI to be beneficial in the long term, Gates emphasizes the need to invest in education and training. This includes reskilling workers whose jobs could be automated, as well as teaching digital skills to younger generations.
3. **Cautious assessment of companies** : Gates encourages investors to evaluate technology companies cautiously. He advises focusing on economic fundamentals and long-term prospects rather than short-term speculative trends.
4. **Innovation continue** : Finally, Gates emphasizes the importance of continuous innovation. Companies must not only develop cutting-edge technologies, but also find practical applications that bring real added value to society.

In sum, Bill Gates strongly believes in the transformative potential of AI, but he calls for a balanced and cautious approach to maximize profits while minimizing the risks of a tech bubble forming.

4.4.3 Alan Greenspan: Lessons from Alan Greenspan's observations of past financial bubbles and how they can apply to AI

Alan Greenspan, former chairman of the US Federal Reserve, is well known for his in-depth analyzes of financial bubbles. His concept of "irrational exuberance" is particularly relevant when examining the warning signs of a bubble in the artificial intelligence (AI) sector.

Observations on Past Bubbles

Greenspan observed that financial bubbles are often characterized by a rapid and unsustainable rise in asset prices, fueled by irrational investor exuberance. For example, during the 1990s, the dot-com bubble saw massive inflation in the prices of technology stocks, far beyond their intrinsic values. This phenomenon has been amplified by accommodative monetary policies, such as low interest rates and an expansion of the money supply.

Greenspan also pointed out that bubbles are difficult to identify in real time. It is often only after their explosion that their existence is confirmed. He noted that central bank attempts to preempt bubbles with modest interest rate hikes have rarely succeeded in averting crises without causing significant economic contractions (Home) (Wikipedia).

Application to the AI sector

Greenspan's lessons can be directly applied to today's AI industry. Here are some key points:

1. **Irrational exuberance** : The AI sector could see overvaluation similar to that seen during past tech bubbles. Investors, excited about the potential of AI, could push valuations well beyond the companies' true value.
2. **Monetary policies and regulations** : Low interest rates and easy access to credit may encourage excessive investment in the AI

sector. However, attempts to regulate or curb these investments must be made carefully to avoid a broader economic contraction.
3. **Precaution and rigorous evaluation** : Greenspan has always advocated a rigorous assessment of economic fundamentals. In the context of AI, this means that investors must scrutinize the business models, revenues and potential profitability of technology companies to avoid falling into the trap of excessive valuations based on unrealistic expectations.
4. **Impact of Investor Psychology** : As with past bubbles, investor psychology plays a crucial role. Irrational optimism can lead to imprudent investments. It is essential to maintain a balanced perspective and be wary of overly optimistic predictions regarding the capabilities of AI and its immediate practical applications (Home) (Cato Institute) (Investopedia).

In summary, Alan Greenspan's observations of past financial bubbles offer valuable lessons for investors and regulators in the AI sector. Vigilance, rigorous evaluation of fundamentals and an understanding of psychological market dynamics are essential to navigating this complex landscape and avoiding the pitfalls of irrational exuberance.

Chapter 5: Stock Market Crash Scenarios

You know, stock market crashes are like those nightmarish dreams that you have a hard time waking up from. They often begin with a gentle euphoria, a feeling that everything is going well in the best of all possible worlds. Prices are soaring, investors are delighted, and the skeptics are made to look like fools. Then, suddenly, everything falls apart. Smiles turn into grimaces, and euphoria gives way to panic. In this chapter, we'll dive into these catastrophic scenarios, exploring how these bubbles burst and what can be done to survive the impact.

5.1 How a bubble bursts

It's funny, you know, how a bubble bursts. It's like that phrase from Robert Frost, "Nothing gold can stay." It all starts with excess optimism. Asset prices are soaring to stratospheric heights, fueled by speculation and the belief that trees reach to the sky. Investors, intoxicated by quick gains, forget economic fundamentals. We buy because everyone buys, and we reassure ourselves by thinking that this time, it's different.

But reality always ends up catching up with fiction. The first signs of weakness appear: a company announces disappointing results, interest rates increase, or new regulation changes the situation. Suddenly, euphoria turns into doubt. Those who were the most optimistic become the first to sell, triggering a cascade of panicked selling. Prices fall as quickly as they rose, and investors find themselves running to salvage what they can of their investments.

Consider the dot-com bubble of the late 1990s. Stocks of technology companies soared to dizzying heights, despite the lack of real profits for many of them. Then, in 2000, the market turned around. Investors realized that valuations were unsustainable. In a matter of months, billions of dollars of market value disappeared, leaving wallets devastated and personal savings wiped out.

In conclusion, a bubble bursts when economic reality takes over. It's a stark reminder that fundamentals still matter, even in times of exuberance. Investors should remain vigilant and remember that all that glitters is not gold.

5.2 Possible scenarios for an AI crisis

Artificial intelligence, despite its promises and potential, is not without risks. AI crisis scenarios can manifest in many ways, highlighting the vulnerabilities inherent in this rapidly expanding technology. This chapter explores the various ways in which a crisis could emerge, focusing on the overvaluation of technology companies, over-reliance on AI technologies, reactions from regulators, disruptions in supply chains, decline in investor confidence and the effects of automation on employment and consumption.

5.2.1 Overvaluation of technology companies

Let's do inne in-depth analysis of how AI company valuations can become excessively high relative to their economic fundamentals, creating a bubble ready to burst.

Financial history is full of examples where the irrational exuberance of investors has led to valuations disconnected from economic reality. AI companies, attracting massive investment because of their promises of technological revolution, can quickly see their stocks soar. However, when these expectations are not met, economic reality sets in and valuations fall sharply, causing significant losses for investors.

For a concrete example: In 2024, shares of several AI companies have reached dizzying heights despite modest revenues, reminiscent of the excesses of the dot-com bubble of the 2000s. For example, shares of some companies, like C3.ai and Palantir , saw their prices rise disproportionately to their actual financial results. According to a report from **Seeking Alpha**, capital investments in AI have often been justified by expectations of future growth rather than current performance, creating a bubble ready to burst when these expectations are not realized (Seeking Alpha) (Startups.co.uk).

Another example: Amazon's colossal investments in AI also add to this dynamic. In 2024, Amazon announced a substantial increase in its capital spending on AI, with a 43% jump in the second quarter, reaching $16.41 billion, up from $1.5 billion in the previous quarter. These investments are primarily aimed at improving cloud services and generative AI infrastructure, joining Google and Microsoft in the race to dominate the AI sector (Enterprise Technology News and Analysis).

Amazon's increased spending, while strategic to strengthen its position in the AI market, could also reduce its profit margins in the short term. Efforts to improve profitability through cost reduction and supply chain efficiencies in its retail division may not be enough to offset the impact of massive investments in AI (Enterprise Technology News and Analysis). Moreover, Amazon's action was sanctioned at the beginning of August 2024 when it announced these massive investments in AI, the action lost 12% in one day. Amazon lost $157 billion in market value[1]..."Even if its short-term profitability must be affected, Amazon has announced it: investments above all else!".

In the same type of excess, we find Nividia, whose market capitalization has tripled in one year, reaching dizzying heights thanks to quarterly revenues which have also tripled. However, this valuation is maintained by future growth expectations that may not materialize. Analysts report that Nvidia is currently trading at 20 times expected revenue for 2025 and 16 times expected revenue for 2026, levels considered unsustainable in the long term by many market experts (InvestorPlace).

This type of overvaluation is reminiscent of the excesses seen during the dot-com bubble of the 2000s, where stock prices rose disproportionately to actual company performance. A sharp correction could occur if high expectations are not met, leading to a significant fall in valuations and significant losses for investors.

---

[1]

https://www.zonebourse.com/cours/action/AMAZON-COM-INC-12864605/actualite/Les-actions-d-Amazon-chutent-en-raison-du-ralentissement-de-la-croissance-des-ventes-en-ligne-47544331/

In short, the overvaluation of AI technology companies presents a major risk for investors and could trigger a financial crisis if valuations are not aligned with economic fundamentals.

Amazon's massive investments and Nvidia's high valuations perfectly illustrate the potential dangers of such dynamics.

5.2.2 Over-reliance on AI technologies

Let's explore the risks associated with overreliance on AI technologies, including vulnerability to cyberattacks and technology failures.

With the rapid rise of artificial intelligence, many businesses find themselves increasingly dependent on this technology for their daily operations. This overreliance can lead to significant risks, particularly in terms of cyberattacks and technological breakdowns.

Cyberattacks pose a growing threat to AI-enabled businesses. AI systems, while advanced, are not immune to vulnerabilities. Hackers can exploit flaws in algorithms or technological infrastructure to infiltrate systems, steal sensitive data or disrupt operations. A successful attack can not only cause direct financial losses, but also damage the company's reputation.

Technology failures are another major risk. AI systems require robust and often expensive infrastructure to operate effectively. Any failure of these infrastructures, whether due to hardware problems, software errors or unforeseen incidents, can cause costly service interruptions and affect productivity.

For a concrete example: Companies like Google have faced significant technology infrastructure challenges, leading to reduced profit margins due to increased capital expenditures to maintain and improve AI capabilities. According to a report from **Seeking Alpha**, Google has had to invest heavily in its data centers and technology infrastructure to meet the growing demand for AI-based services, which has weighed on its profit margins (Enterprise Technology News and Analysis).

This situation illustrates the challenges that businesses may face due to their increased reliance on AI technologies. Infrastructure maintenance and improvement costs can increase significantly, reducing profit margins. Additionally, any failure in these systems can result in costly downtime and damage to the company's reputation.

In conclusion, over-reliance on AI technologies carries significant risks for businesses. Cyberattacks and technology failures can have serious consequences, both financial and reputational. Companies must therefore take steps to secure their systems and invest in robust and resilient infrastructure to minimize these risks.

5.2.3 Regulator reactions and market impacts

We are going to analyze regulatory actions taken by governments and their potential effects on financial markets and technology companies.

Regulators play a crucial role in managing and overseeing the adoption of AI technologies. Faced with growing concerns about data privacy, algorithmic bias, and security, governments around the world have begun to implement strict regulations to govern the use of AI. For example, the European Union introduced the AI Act, legislation aimed at regulating high-risk AI systems, by imposing fundamental rights impact assessments and transparency obligations (Seeking Alpha).

Market impact: These regulations, while essential to ensure responsible use of AI, can also have negative effects on the market. They can increase technology companies' operational costs, reduce their flexibility and slow down innovation. For example, new regulatory requirements may require companies to revise their algorithms, invest more in compliance, and face longer timelines for new product launches. This can slow growth and affect stock market valuations.

Regulations can also influence investor perceptions. Increased oversight and strict regulations may be seen as obstacles to the rapid growth potential of AI companies, leading to a reassessment of risks and a decline in investor confidence. For example, following the announcement of new European regulations, the shares of several AI companies fell, reflecting market concerns about the long-term impacts of these regulations on profitability and innovation (Startups.co.uk).

In summary, while regulations are crucial to ensuring ethical and responsible use of AI, they can also pose significant challenges for technology companies and negatively influence financial markets. Businesses must carefully navigate this complex regulatory landscape to balance compliance and innovation.

5.2.4 Disruption of semiconductor supply chains

The increased reliance on semiconductors in the development and expansion of artificial intelligence (AI) technologies poses significant risk if supply chains are disrupted. Semiconductors are essential for powering the complex algorithms and computational infrastructure needed for AI applications. However, various geopolitical and economic tensions can seriously affect this critical supply chain.

Geopolitical vulnerabilities

Growing tensions between the United States and China have already impacted the semiconductor sector. US sanctions against China and restrictions on the export of advanced technologies have disrupted the global chip market. China, in response, has stepped up efforts to develop its own semiconductor industry, but it will take time to significantly reduce its dependence on U.S. and European imports (Enterprise Technology News and Analysis) .

Concrete example: Impact on Nvidia and ASML

Nvidia, a leading AI chip maker, was directly impacted by these disruptions. The company's ability to supply high-performance chips has been hampered by export restrictions and sanctions against Chinese suppliers. As a result, Nvidia's shares have fluctuated in response to news about trade regulations and international tensions (Enterprise Technology News and Analysis) .

ASML, a Dutch company specializing in lithography equipment for semiconductor manufacturing, has also been impacted by export restrictions imposed by the United States. ASML supplies crucial machinery for producing the most advanced chips, and any disruption to their supply chain can have ripple effects across the entire tech industry (Enterprise Technology News and Analysis) .

Economic consequences

Disruptions in the semiconductor supply chain can lead to production delays, increased costs and lower profit margins for technology companies. The massive investments needed to secure and diversify chip supply sources add additional financial pressure on companies. For example, Amazon recently increased its capital spending by 43% to bolster its AI capabilities, with much of that budget dedicated to securing its semiconductor supplies.

Long-term impacts

In the long term, continued geopolitical tensions and supply chain disruptions could slow innovation in the AI sector. Companies may be forced to review their investment strategies, focusing more on resilience and supplier diversification rather than rapid expansion of their technological capabilities.

In conclusion, the disruption of semiconductor supply chains represents a major risk for the AI sector. Geopolitical tensions, trade restrictions, and overreliance on specific vendors must be carefully managed to avoid potentially devastating crises in the technology industry.

5.2.5 Decline in investor confidence

Investor confidence is a fundamental pillar of financial markets. When it falters, the consequences can be disastrous for company valuations, particularly in a booming sector like artificial intelligence (AI). Declining investor confidence can manifest itself in several ways and lead to a series of chain reactions that exacerbate the crisis.

AI Bubble: How to Survive the Next Stock Market Crash

Declining investor confidence occurs when high expectations about future business performance are not met. In the context of AI, this loss of trust can be triggered by disappointing earnings reports, technology scandals, restrictive regulations or geopolitical events. When investors lose confidence, they begin to sell their stocks, which can cause prices to fall rapidly and increase volatility in the markets.

For a concrete example: In 2024, several large technology companies, including those specializing in AI, saw their shares fall after announcing quarterly results that were below expectations. For example, Nvidia, despite a 262% year-over-year increase in revenue, saw its shares fall 5% due to concerns about the sustainability of this exceptional growth and more modest forecasts for the years to come ([Enterprise Technology News and Analysis](#)). Similarly, Amazon also felt similar pressure after announcing a substantial increase in its capital spending on AI, thereby reducing its short-term profit margins ([Enterprise Technology News and Analysis](#)).

Market analysts and institutional investors play a crucial role in these dynamics. When influential entities start issuing negative reviews or lowering their forecasts for key companies in the AI sector, it can trigger a chain reaction. Individual investors often follow these signals, exacerbating sell-offs and falling stock prices.

The increased volatility that accompanies loss of confidence may also have broader market implications. Technology companies, being often interconnected by supply chains and strategic partnerships, may see their valuations affected by declining trust in a single major player. For example, stocks of semiconductor and cloud service providers may also fall if the outlook for AI leaders becomes uncertain.

In conclusion, declining investor confidence in the AI sector can have devastating effects. It not only diminishes the value of individual companies, but it can also cause broader instability in financial markets. For businesses, it is crucial to maintain transparent communication and manage expectations realistically to avoid such a crisis of trust.

5.2.6 Effects of automation on employment and consumption

Automation powered by artificial intelligence (AI) is having profound impacts on the labor market and consumption levels. This subchapter examines how the growing adoption of AI to automate tasks is influencing employment and, therefore, overall consumption, creating unique challenges and opportunities.

Impact on employment

Automation through AI is transforming the nature of work by eliminating some jobs while creating new ones. According to a McKinsey report, around 375 million workers worldwide may need to change job categories by 2030 due to automation and AI【McKinsey Global Institute】. The hardest hit industries include manufacturing, retail, and administrative services, where many repetitive tasks are easily automated.

- **For a concrete example:** In the retail industry, companies like Amazon are using inventory management systems and sorting robots to automate tasks once done by human workers. This reduces the demand for unskilled labor while increasing operational efficiency.
- **New jobs:** Although some jobs are disappearing, AI is also creating new opportunities in areas such as software development, maintenance of AI systems, and data analysis. For example, "data scientist" and "machine learning specialist" positions are seeing increasing demand.

Impact on consumption

Changes in employment directly affect consumption, because workers' disposable income influences their purchasing habits. Loss of jobs or reduced working hours due to automation may lead to lower consumption in certain regions or sectors.

- **Economic inequality:** Automation can exacerbate economic inequality. Workers whose skills are supplemented by AI often

see their income increase, while those whose skills are replaced by AI may face significant income losses.
- **For a concrete example:** An OECD report says low-skilled workers are most vulnerable to job loss due to automation, which could lead to reduced consumption in market segments that rely on this population【OECD】.

Retraining and training initiatives

To mitigate the negative effects of automation, many companies and governments are investing in reskilling and training programs. The goal is to prepare workers for new opportunities created by the digital economy.

- **For a concrete example:** In 2023, Amazon launched a training program called "Upskill 2025," aiming to train 100,000 employees in the advanced technology skills needed for the jobs of tomorrow. This type of program helps mitigate the effects of job loss due to automation by providing opportunities for workers to move into more technical, higher-paying roles【Amazon Press Release】.

Long-term economic consequences

In the long term, automation could lead to a significant restructuring of the global economy. If reskilling and training programs are successful, they could lead to a more skilled and adaptable workforce capable of leveraging new technologies to drive economic growth. However, if inequalities are not addressed, automation could also lead to social and economic instability.

In conclusion, the effects of automation on employment and consumption are complex and multifaceted. They require sustained attention from policymakers, businesses and educators to ensure that the benefits of AI are shared equitably and that workers are prepared for the challenges of the future.

5.3 Comparison with previous crashes

Financial bubbles and stock market crashes have marked economic history on several occasions. To better understand possible scenarios for an AI-related crisis, it is instructive to compare this situation with previous crashes. Here is a detailed analysis of several historical events and the lessons that can be learned from them.

But first, as some analysts or economics professors are quite keen on the nuances of Krach, let's see how we could classify these financial crises in relation to their defined category:

Definition of Terms

- **Krach Boursier** : A sharp and significant drop in stock prices on one or more stock exchanges within a short period of time, often caused by investor panic and underlying economic factors. The drop is generally greater than 20%.
- **Flash Crash** : A rapid and deep fall in asset prices, followed by an equally rapid recovery, often caused by trading errors, algorithms, or momentary market events.
- **Correction** : A decline of 10% or more in asset prices from their recent peak, generally considered a healthy and normal revaluation in a bull market.

5.3.1 Railway Mania (1842-1848)

The Railway Mania in the United Kingdom in the 1840s is a classic example of a speculative bubble. Railway company shares saw their prices double between 1843 and 1845. The enthusiasm for investment in railways was such that even unviable projects received massive financing. This bubble burst in 1848, causing huge losses for investors and a prolonged economic crisis. The key factors were excessive speculation, unregulated investments and an overvaluation of assets relative to their real value (Liberty Street Economics) (The Big Picture).

- **Classification** : Krach Boursier

5.3.2 Overvaluation crashes (1987 and 1998)

In 1987, "Black Monday" saw the global stock market fall sharply in a single day, mainly due to overvaluation of stocks and investor panic. In 1998, the Asian financial crisis led to high market volatility, exacerbated by the bankruptcy of the LTCM fund. These events show how excessive valuations and investor overconfidence can quickly turn into panic and market collapse (Liberty Street Economics).

- **1987**
    - **Classification** : Krach Boursier
    - **Description** : "Black Monday" of October 19, 1987 was characterized by a sudden and significant fall in world markets in a single day. Investor panic and automatic selling caused the Dow to drop 22%.
- **1998**
    - **Classification** : Correction
    - **Description** : The fall was not as brutal or immediate as that of 1987. The drop was significant but spread over a longer period, characteristic of a correction.

5.3.3 Telecommunications bubble (2000-2001)

The telecommunications bubble, also known as the dot-com bubble, was fueled by massive investments in internet startups and telecommunications infrastructure. When companies failed to generate profits, the bubble burst, leading to the bankruptcy of many companies and a drastic fall in stock markets. This crash highlights the dangers of investing based on speculative expectations rather than solid economic fundamentals (Wikipedia) (Cambridge University Press & Assessment).

- **Classification** : Krach Boursier
- **Description** : The sudden drop in technology valuations over a short period qualifies this event as a crash.

5.3.4 Faillite de Lehman Brothers (2008)

The bankruptcy of Lehman Brothers in 2008 triggered a global financial crisis. The subprime crisis led to a massive accumulation of toxic debt in the financial system. The fall of Lehman caused a banking panic and a freeze in credit markets, leading to a global recession. This event illustrates the systemic risks posed by the interconnectedness of financial institutions and the cascading effects of failures (Liberty Street Economics).

- **Classification** : Krach Boursier
- **Description** : The banking panic and the freezing of credit markets caused a systemic collapse, typical of a crash.

5.3.5 Greek debt crisis (2011)

The Greek debt crisis in 2011 exposed the vulnerabilities of highly indebted economies and the challenges of managing sovereign debt in a monetary union. Austerity measures imposed in response to the crisis caused social unrest and a prolonged recession in Greece, also affecting European financial markets. This shows how debt crises can have significant impacts on regional and global economies (Liberty Street Economics).

- **Classification** : Correction
- **Description** : Market declines, while significant, occurred over a prolonged period, more characteristic of a correction.

5.3.6 USA/China economic war (December 2018)

The 2018 US-China trade war led to significant disruptions to global supply chains and increased market uncertainty. Tariffs and trade retaliations have affected many sectors, demonstrating how geopolitical tensions can trigger global economic and financial turmoil (The Big Picture).

- **Classification** : Correction
- **Description** : The resulting market declines, while notable, did not have the brutality or speed of a crash, falling more into the category of corrections.

5.3.7 COVID-19 pandemic (March 2020)

The COVID-19 pandemic has caused one of the fastest and most severe stock market declines in history. Global lockdowns and economic disruptions have led to a global recession, requiring unprecedented interventions by governments and central banks to stabilize markets and support economies. This event shows how unforeseen external shocks can have devastating impacts on financial markets (The Big Picture).

- **Classification** : Krach Boursier
- **Description** : This sudden fall in the markets in a few weeks, requiring unprecedented interventions to stabilize the global economy, is undoubtedly a stock market crash.

Conclusion

Each stock market crash and financial crisis has its own characteristics, but common themes emerge: excessive speculation, overvaluations, irrational investor confidence, and inadequate responses to warning signs.

By comparing the potential AI bubble with these past crises, we can better anticipate warning signs and potential impacts, while developing strategies to mitigate risks and manage crises more effectively.

Looking more closely at these past events, we can find worrying similarities with the current situation around Artificial Intelligence (AI).

AI Bubble: How to Survive the Next Stock Market Crash

Take, for example, the **1840s Railway Mania**. Speculation about railway companies led to massive overvaluation of stocks, reaching heights disconnected from economic reality. It was only once the bubble burst in 1848 that investors realized the extent of their collective blindness. Similarly, today, AI companies are seeing their valuations skyrocket. Promises of extraordinary returns and technological revolutions captivate investors, even as delays and technical challenges begin to emerge.

In 1987, the **crash of "Black Monday"** illustrated how investor panic can turn a correction into a total collapse. That day, a brutal 22% fall in the Dow Jones highlighted the vulnerability of markets to panic. Today, a severe correction in the AI sector could easily trigger a similar chain reaction, exacerbated by the volatility inherent in these new technologies.

The **telecommunications bubble of the 2000s** also offers striking parallels. At the time, internet start-ups were valued well beyond their actual profit-generating capabilities. When these companies began to fail, the bubble burst, causing the markets to fall drastically. Likewise, AI companies, despite their impressive advancements, may fail to meet investors' high expectations, leading to a comparable crash.

The **bankruptcy of Lehman Brothers in 2008** recalls the dangers of toxic debt and complex interconnections in the financial system. The subprime crisis has revealed how structural flaws can lead to bank runs and frozen credit markets. AI companies, often backed by massive funding and expectations of rapid growth, could see their own financial structures tested in difficult market conditions.

In 2011, the **Greek debt crisis** showed how over-indebted economies can cause major social and economic unrest. Current geopolitical tensions, particularly between the United States and China, are exacerbating vulnerabilities around AI technologies. Sanctions, restrictions and national rivalries create a climate of uncertainty that could easily destabilize markets.

The **economic war between the United States and China in 2018** demonstrated the impact of geopolitical tensions on global markets. Supply chain disruptions and trade uncertainty have caused significant economic turmoil. Likewise, technological dominance and battles over AI add a layer of complexity to current economic risks.

Finally, the **COVID-19 pandemic in 2020** showed how an unforeseen external shock can have devastating impacts on financial markets. The rapid and severe fall in markets in March 2020 required unprecedented interventions by governments and central banks to stabilize the economy. If an AI bubble were to burst, similar interventions may be necessary to avoid total collapse.

In summary, the hallmarks of past crises – excessive overvaluations, investor panic, technological failures, geopolitical tensions, and central bank interventions – are present in the current AI context. These similarities suggest that we may be on the cusp of a new era of financial volatility and instability, unless prudent measures and appropriate regulations are put in place to mitigate these risks.

Chapter 6: Anticipation scenario for an AI-related crisis

This anticipatory scenario, although pure fiction, illustrates how fragile the balance of our global economy is. With today's already tense environment – from geopolitical tensions to volatile financial markets to rapid technological advancements – this story highlights the potential vulnerabilities we could face. By exploring a hypothetical crisis linked to Artificial Intelligence during the winter of 2024-25, this story invites us to reflect on the consequences of speculative excesses and the importance of prudence and regulation in a constantly evolving world.

6.1 Economic and financial context

In 2024 and 2025, the US Federal Reserve's (FED) repeated promises to cut interest rates to stimulate the economy were continually postponed until it was too late. The already fragile global economy is entering a phase of severe slowdown, particularly affecting the United States and China. In China, the real estate crisis is worsening, leading to a fall in domestic demand and exports, exacerbating trade tensions with the United States.

The sublime seven tech giants – Amazon, Google, Microsoft, Apple, Meta, Nvidia, and Tesla – have all invested heavily in artificial intelligence, anticipating exponential returns. Amazon has allocated more than $60 billion to improve its cloud services and generative AI infrastructure, hoping to overtake rivals Google and Microsoft. However, revenues from these new technologies have failed to offset declines in their core activities: goods sales for Amazon and advertising revenues for Google.

6.2 The Spark of Infatuation

The winter of 2024-25 was shaping up to be the most promising in the history of financial markets. Artificial Intelligence (AI) technologies had permeated every corner of the global economy. From New York to Tokyo,

Paris and Shanghai, investors were captivated by the meteoric rise of AI companies. The whole world seemed hypnotized by the promises of this new technological era.

The tech giants had seen their valuations skyrocket. AI start-ups, even those without concrete products, were attracting millions in venture capital. Governments, eager not to be left behind in this technological race, were taking on heavily more debt to finance infrastructure and research programs in AI. The speculative frenzy reached a fever pitch when NexoNet, a promising company, announced a strategic partnership with several governments to deploy AI solutions on a large scale.

6.3 The Heat of Illusion

The first cracks appeared at the beginning of December 2024. NexoNet, symbol of this revolution, made an unexpected announcement: significant delays in the development of its flagship AI, caused by unforeseen technological obstacles. This news hit like a bombshell. Financial analysts, until then optimistic, began to doubt the viability of the excessive valuations that had accumulated.

In January 2025, interest rates, unable to fall to stimulate the economy, were, on the contrary, suddenly increased by central banks. This decision, motivated by once again galloping inflation and pressure on national currencies, made debt service unsustainable for many companies and states. The debts incurred to finance the AI race became a crushing burden.

6.4 The Health Crisis: the "Helion Flu" Virus

Alongside these economic upheavals, a new health crisis is breaking out. An extremely virulent virus, nicknamed the "Helion Flu", appears. Similar to avian flu, this virus spreads quickly in high-density urban areas. Symptoms include severe hemorrhagic fever and alarming mortality rates.

The health crisis is worsening the economic situation, paralyzing cities and disrupting global supply chains.

6.5 The Bursting of the Bubble

On February 10, 2025, the announcement by one of the largest investment banks of the liquidation of its positions in AI companies had the effect of an earthquake. Investors, panicked, began selling en masse. Stock market indices fell spectacularly. AI companies, once darlings of the markets, saw their value plummet. The highly exposed hedge funds found themselves bankrupt. Banks, faced with assets that had become toxic, suddenly tightened credit conditions.

The reasons for this collapse were multiple:

- **Excessive Overvaluations** : The valuations of AI companies had become disproportionate to their economic fundamentals.
- **Massive Debt** : States and companies had contracted colossal debts to finance this technological bubble.
- **Increase in Interest Rates** : The sudden rise in rates made the debt burden unbearable.
- **Loss of Confidence** : Delays and failures of AI projects undermine investor confidence.

6.6 Repercussions

The repercussions of this collapse were devastating:

- **Interest Rates and Debt** : Rates continued to rise, worsening the deficits of already overindebted states. Sovereign credit ratings were downgraded, eroding confidence in bond markets.
- **Loss of Value and Recession** : Stock markets, having lost a large part of their value, plunged the world economy into a deep

recession. Companies cut spending and laid off workers en masse.
- **Crisis of Confidence** : Confidence in governments and the financial system was severely compromised. Populist movements, fueled by popular anger, gained power, threatening political stability.

6.7 Epilogue: Reconstruction

In the months that followed, the world found itself facing a period of reconstruction. Financial regulations were strengthened to prevent future speculative bubbles. The lessons learned from this crisis pushed towards more sustainable innovation and balanced growth. But the scars left by this tumultuous winter remained etched in the collective memory, reminding us of the dangers of greed and illusion.

Thus, the winter of 2024-25 was marked by the spectacular bursting of the AI bubble, a time when the most ambitious dreams collided with harsh economic reality, leaving behind a world in search of renewal and caution.

Thank God this is only fiction and the dates will undoubtedly have passed by the time you read these lines...

Chapter 7: Are we in a crash scenario in 2024, in real life?

7.1 Context and Economic Conditions since July 2024

7.1.1 The real current context (in August 2024)

Since July 2024, the financial markets have been going through a tumultuous period. The Nasdaq, representing technology stocks, has already fallen significantly, mainly due to concerns about overvaluations of Artificial Intelligence (AI) companies. The decline came after a strong advance in June, when enthusiasm for AI technologies pushed valuations to record highs.

7.1.2 The Causes of the Decline

- **Overvaluations of AI Companies** : AI companies have seen their valuations inflate beyond their economic fundamentals. Promises of exponential growth attracted massive investment, but the reality of technological delays and high costs began to erode investor confidence.
- **Monetary Policies** : The US Federal Reserve (FED) has been criticized for being slow to lower interest rates. This inertia has maintained a high interest rate environment, making financing more expensive and weighing on overindebted companies, particularly in the technology sector.
- **Geopolitical Tensions** : Geopolitical tensions around technological dominance and AI, notably between the United States and China, have added to the uncertainty. Sanctions and

restrictions on exports of critical technologies have disrupted supply chains and exacerbated recession fears.

7.1.3 The July Correction

In July 2024, a severe correction in the Nasdaq took place, marked by a decline in the valuations of technology companies. This correction, while necessary to realign prices with fundamentals, has intensified fears of a broader collapse. Investors have become more cautious, reducing their positions in high-risk assets.

7.1.4 The Hope and Reality of Rates

The hope of a rate cut by the FED remains a hot topic. Although some FED officials have indicated a possible rate cut to support the economy, concrete action is slow to come. This wait creates additional uncertainty in the markets, slowing the recovery of investments and exacerbating financial tensions.

7.1.5 Conclusion

The contemporary situation is marked by high volatility and persistent uncertainties. The combination of technological overvaluations, geopolitical tensions, and hesitant monetary policies poses a considerable challenge for investors. The ability of markets to stabilize will largely depend on the reaction of the FED and the evolution of international tensions around AI.

7.2 The Nikkei Crash of August 5, 2024

On August 5, 2024, the Nikkei, Japan's flagship stock index, suffered a spectacular crash with a fall of 5.8%. This event, although significant, should not be immediately interpreted as a precursor to the bursting of an Artificial Intelligence (AI) bubble. It is crucial to understand the contexts and dynamics at play to assess the true impact of this incident on global markets.

7.2.1 A Sign of Weakness or a Prelude to a Crisis?

The Nikkei's fall was mainly caused by a second consecutive interest rate hike by the Bank of Japan. This increase had the immediate effect of strengthening the yen, which penalized Japanese exporters and, consequently, the entire stock market. Furthermore, the contraction of the PMI indices in Europe and the United States has increased investor nervousness. This macroeconomic data has fueled fears of an impending global recession.

However, this event must be put into perspective. Financial markets are inherently volatile and prone to severe corrections, especially after periods of strong growth. The Nikkei crash could be interpreted as a reaction to a combination of short-term adverse economic factors, rather than a surefire indicator of an impending collapse of the AI bubble.

7.2.2 Implications for the AI Bubble

AI technologies, although revolutionary, are not immune to global economic dynamics. The central question is whether current valuations of AI companies are sustainable in the long term or whether they reflect a speculative bubble. The global economic slowdown and monetary policy adjustments can certainly pose challenges, but they do not necessarily mean the collapse of a sector.

Yet excessive enthusiasm around AI, without strong economic fundamentals, could actually precipitate a crisis if expectations are not realized. Investors must therefore be vigilant and prepare for a possible market correction, while recognizing that technological innovation continues to represent immense potential.

7.2.3 Lessons to Learn

- **Cautious Analysis** : The Nikkei crash should be seen as a wake-up call, prompting a more cautious analysis of investments in AI technologies.
- **Diversification** : Diversified portfolios can better withstand economic shocks and avoid excessive exposure to a single sector.
- **Monitoring Monetary Policies** : Central bank decisions have a significant impact on financial markets. It is crucial to follow these developments to anticipate market movements.

In conclusion, the Nikkei crash of August 5, 2024 highlights the current fragility of financial markets, but it should not be seen as definitive proof of the imminent bursting of the AI bubble. A balanced and vigilant approach remains key to navigating this period of economic uncertainty.

Chapter 8: Consequences of a Stock Market Crash

The bursting of a financial bubble is a dramatic event that can have profound and lasting repercussions on the global economy. A stock market crash doesn't just reduce the value of investment portfolios; it can also cause a series of chain reactions that affect businesses, governments and households. In this chapter, we will explore the potential consequences of an AI-related stock market crash, starting with its overall economic impact.

8.1 Overall economic impact

A stock market crash can cause a series of economic shocks that ripple across the world. When financial markets collapse, investor confidence evaporates, leading to reduced investment and consumer spending. Businesses, facing lower demand and tighter credit conditions, may cut investments, lay off workers and, in extreme cases, declare bankruptcy.

Reduction of investments : Falling stock markets often lead to a significant reduction in capital investments. Companies, faced with a loss in the value of their shares and a reduction in their financial resources, are postponing or canceling their expansion plans. This can slow innovation and economic growth in the long term.

Increase in unemployment : Companies in financial difficulty may be forced to reduce their workforce to survive. The resulting mass layoffs increase the unemployment rate, which reduces household purchasing power and further deepens the economic recession.

Business failures : The most vulnerable companies, especially those that rely heavily on financial markets for financing, may not survive a stock market crash. The resulting wave of bankruptcies can have devastating effects on entire economic sectors and lead to massive job losses.

Effects on the financial system : Banks and other financial institutions can suffer significant losses due to the devaluation of the assets they hold. This can lead to a liquidity crisis, where banks become reluctant to lend, exacerbating economic difficulties.

Government interventions : Governments and central banks often intervene to stabilize financial markets and support the economy. These interventions may include interest rate cuts, economic stimulus programs, and bailouts of large businesses or financial institutions. Although these measures can mitigate the immediate effects of a crash, they can also increase public debt and create long-term economic distortions.

Worldwide impact : In a globalized economy, a stock market crash in one region can have global repercussions. International supply chains, capital flows and trade relationships can all be disrupted, leading to a global economic recession.

A stock market crash linked to artificial intelligence could have devastating economic consequences, affecting not only financial markets but also the real economy across the world. Policymakers, businesses and investors must be prepared to face these challenges to mitigate negative impacts and foster a rapid and sustainable recovery.

When the market crashes, the effects are immediate and profound. An economic recession is almost inevitable. Falling stock values reduce the wealth of households and businesses, leading to lower consumption and investment. Companies, suddenly faced with plummeting demand, are cutting spending and laying off employees. This downward spiral further deepens the recession, making recovery all the more difficult.

Consumer and investor confidence is taking a severe hit. People become cautious with their money, preferring to save rather than spend or invest. This loss of confidence translates into reduced consumption and excessive caution, which hampers economic growth. Investors, scalded by market volatility, avoid risks, which limits the flow of capital towards innovative or risky projects.

The increase in unemployment is a direct consequence of this situation. Companies, to survive the crisis, are cutting their workforce. The unemployment rate is rising, which has ripple effects on aggregate demand and social stability. Families affected by unemployment reduce their spending, which affects other sectors of the economy, creating a vicious cycle of economic decline.

Banks and financial institutions are also being hit hard. Their stock portfolios are suffering colossal losses, which limits their ability to lend. **A liquidity crisis sets in**, and if key institutions fail, it can cause a domino effect throughout the financial system. The credit crunch is suffocating businesses and households, further aggravating the crisis.

When it comes to inflation or deflation, it all depends on how governments and central banks react. If monetary policies are too expansive to counter the recession, inflation may appear. Conversely, sluggish demand can lead to deflationary pressure, where prices fall continuously, which is no longer desirable.

Public finances are also suffering the repercussions of a stock market crash. Tax revenues fall due to lower capital gains and dividends, while government spending increases to support the unemployed and revive the economy. This dual pressure can widen budget deficits and increase public debt, limiting governments' capacity for future intervention.

In short, a stock market crash is not just a market crisis; it is a shock wave that shakes the entire global economy, affecting individuals, businesses, and governments in profound and lasting ways. The ability to respond quickly and effectively to such events is crucial to limiting damage and fostering economic recovery.

8.2 Effects on Technology Companies and Investors

When an Artificial Intelligence (AI) bubble bursts, the repercussions are particularly severe for technology companies that have invested heavily in this technology. These companies, which have benefited from valuations inflated by high expectations for future growth, see their value plummet when reality catches up with optimistic projections.

For Technology Companies:

Tech companies are on the front lines when an AI bubble bursts. Meta, Google, Microsoft, and other tech giants, having invested billions in AI projects, suffer colossal losses when their investments do not materialize as quickly as expected. For example, delays in the development of AI technologies or unforeseen obstacles can lead to a rapid drop in investor confidence (EL PAÍS English).

As a result, these companies must face a drastic reduction in their financing. Banks, having become cautious after suffering losses on stock portfolios, are limiting their loans, which is forcing technology companies to reduce their spending and put many innovation projects on hold. Mass layoffs are becoming inevitable, worsening unemployment in the tech sector and beyond.

Technology company revenues are also affected by a decrease in demand. Consumers and businesses, hit by the recession, are reducing their spending on new technologies, exacerbating the financial difficulties of AI companies. Promises of future earnings turn into financial burdens as businesses must manage high costs with declining revenues.

For Investors:

Investors in AI companies are suffering massive losses. Increased volatility and rapid declines in stock prices are causing widespread panic. Many investors, in panic, sell at a loss to avoid even more pronounced falls, which amplifies the fall in the markets.

Investment funds and pension funds, often heavily exposed to technology stocks, are seeing the value of their portfolios fall drastically. This situation directly affects returns for investors and retirees who rely on these funds for their income (markets.businessinsider.com).

For individual investors, the losses can be even more dramatic. Life savings can melt away in a matter of days or weeks, reducing their ability to consume and invest in the economy. Confidence in financial markets is severely shaken, and many investors are reluctant to return to the markets, fearing a repeat of the collapse (EL PAÍS English) (markets.businessinsider.com).

In summary, the bursting of the AI bubble has devastating consequences for technology companies and their investors. Businesses must navigate between immediate survival and preparation for eventual recovery, as investors attempt to minimize their losses in a highly volatile market environment. These dynamics reinforce overall economic difficulties and prolong the recovery period after a crash.

8.3 Consequences for the Real Economy

The bursting of the Artificial Intelligence (AI) bubble is not limited to financial markets and technology companies. The repercussions are felt deeply in the real economy, affecting various sectors, households, and overall socio-economic stability.

Impact on Employment and the Labor Market

One of the immediate consequences of an AI-related stock market crash is increased unemployment. Tech companies, by downsizing to survive the crisis, are freeing up a skilled workforce that is struggling to find new opportunities in a saturated market. This phenomenon is not limited to technology workers alone; The effects of the recession also affect adjacent industries such as marketing, sales and services, which rely heavily on spending by technology companies.

Reduction of Consumption

The loss of wealth due to the fall in stock markets leads to a significant reduction in household consumption. Individuals, seeing their savings and investments dwindle, are adopting a more conservative approach and reducing their discretionary spending. This drop in consumption is affecting many sectors, from retail to real estate, the automotive industry and leisure.

Contraction of Investments

Companies, including those outside the technology sector, are becoming more cautious in their expansion plans. Investment projects are postponed or canceled, and capital expenditures are reduced. This contraction in investment hampers innovation and long-term economic growth. Sectors like construction, infrastructure, and even research and development (R&D) are seeing their budgets cut, slowing technological and economic progress.

Financial and Credit Instability

Banks and financial institutions, already reeling from market losses, are becoming extremely reluctant to lend. This liquidity crisis seriously affects small and medium-sized enterprises (SMEs) which depend on bank loans for their current operations and expansions. The credit crunch is causing a wave of bankruptcies among SMEs, which further increases unemployment and economic recession.

Deflation and Price Pressure

The recession following the bursting of the AI bubble may lead to deflationary pressure. Declining aggregate demand causes prices of goods and services to fall, which at first glance may seem beneficial to consumers. However, deflation increases the real debt burden and can lead to a deflationary spiral where consumption and investment continue to decline, exacerbating the recession.

Public Finances and Budget Deficits

Governments are seeing their tax revenues fall due to lower capital gains, dividends, and corporate taxes. At the same time, public spending is increasing to support the unemployed and revive the economy through economic stimulation programs. This situation leads to increased budget deficits and an increase in public debt, limiting the ability of governments to intervene effectively in future crises.

Social and Political Tensions

Rising unemployment and economic insecurity are fueling social tensions. Protest movements may emerge, demanding economic reforms and better social protection. Economic inequalities, exacerbated by the crisis, can lead to political instabilities and a rise in populist movements, endangering social cohesion and political stability.

In summary, the bursting of the AI bubble has profound and lasting consequences on the real economy. The ensuing cascade of economic, social, and political problems illustrates the extent to which a speculative bubble can destabilize the entire economic system and affect the daily lives of millions of people.

Chapter 9: Anticipating and Detecting a Crash

9.1 Strategies for Detecting an Impending Crash

Detecting an imminent crash, particularly in the context of an Artificial Intelligence (AI) bubble, requires a combination of strategic approaches and diverse analyses. It is not enough to monitor financial and economic indicators; it is also necessary to take a broader perspective and use various tools and techniques to anticipate the warning signs of a crisis.

1. Continued Monitoring for Signs of Overvaluation

A key strategy is to maintain constant vigilance on AI company valuations. This involves regularly comparing the valuation ratios (such as the P/E ratio) of technology companies with their historical averages and those of the overall market. Significant divergence may indicate a bubble in the making.

2. Use of Technical Analysis

Technical analysis can provide valuable insights by detecting chart patterns that often precede market reversals. Investors should pay attention to sell signals like bearish moving average crossovers, head-and-shoulders patterns, and trendline breaks. These tools can help anticipate corrections before they become major crashes.

3. Application of Advanced Quantitative Models

Quantitative forecasting models use sophisticated algorithms to analyze large amounts of historical and current data. By incorporating variables specific to AI companies and the technology sector, these models can provide more accurate predictions on market movements. Using artificial intelligence itself to predict crash risks can provide a competitive advantage.

4. Monitoring the Activities of Institutional Investors

The movements of large institutional investors can be leading indicators. An effective strategy is to monitor the position reports of pension funds, sovereign wealth funds, and large investment banks. Heavy sales or significant reductions in positions in technology stocks can signal a loss of confidence in the sector.

5. Sentiment Analysis and Social Media

Investor and consumer sentiments, often reflected in social media and online forums, can offer early clues to market psychology. Sentiment analysis tools can help quantify general optimism or pessimism toward AI technologies. A sudden increase in negative talk or crash predictions may indicate growing nervousness.

6. Diversification of Portfolios

To protect against the risk of an AI-related crash, investors should diversify their portfolios. Diversifying across different sectors and asset classes reduces exposure to the specific risk of a tech bubble. Investments in defensive assets like bonds or commodities can provide a hedge against market falls.

7. Monitoring of Government and Regulatory Policies

Political and regulatory decisions can have a significant impact on technology markets. A proactive strategy is to monitor announcements and regulatory changes that could affect AI companies. New data privacy laws, trade restrictions, and economic sanctions can all play a crucial role.

8. Scenario Simulation and Stress Tests

Scenario simulations and stress tests are essential tools for assessing the resilience of a portfolio in the face of various economic shocks. By modeling different crash scenarios, investors can identify potential vulnerabilities and adjust their strategies accordingly. These exercises make it possible to prepare contingency plans to react quickly in the event of a crisis.

9. Monitoring of Technological Innovations

Finally, continued monitoring of technological innovations in the field of AI can provide clues about the direction of the market. Major technological advances or failures can influence investor expectations. A thorough understanding of technology trends helps anticipate periods of euphoria or disappointment that may precede a crash.

By combining these strategies, investors can better anticipate the risks of a stock market crash linked to the bursting of the AI bubble. A proactive and diversified approach, based on rigorous analysis and the use of advanced tools, is essential to navigate a volatile and complex market environment.

9.2 Use of Financial and Economic Indicators

To anticipate and detect a stock market crash linked to the bursting of the Artificial Intelligence (AI) bubble, it is crucial to use a variety of financial and economic indicators. These indicators make it possible to measure the health of the market and identify potential imbalances before they turn into major crises.

Here is an analysis of the main indicators that can signal an imminent stock market crash and where we are today in August 2024 for each of these indicators:

1. Excessively High Price/Earnings (P/E) Ratio

A very high P/E ratio compared to historical averages may indicate an overvaluation of the market. When investors pay exorbitant prices for stocks relative to the profits generated, it can signal a speculative bubble.

- Current: The P/E ratio of the S&P 500 Index is currently at 27.45, which is significantly above the historical average of 16.08 and even the last 5 years average of 20.30. This high level indicates a significant overvaluation of the market (World PE Ratio) (Multpl).

2. Market Volatility (VIX Index)

The VIX, often called the "fear index," measures expected market volatility. A sudden increase in the VIX may indicate rising nervousness among investors, which may precede a crash.

- **Current** : The VIX is currently at 38.57, which is a high level and indicates strong nervousness among investors (YCharts). During the Nikkei crash on August 5, 2024, the Cboe Volatility Index (VIX), soared 64.9% to its highest level since March 2020. This surge in the VIX reflects increased nervousness among investors and is an indicator of the extreme volatility of financial markets at that time (Schaeffers Investment Research) (Coinspeaker).

3. Divergence of Moving Averages

Moving averages are trend indicators. If the short-term moving average crosses below the long-term moving average (bearish crossover), this can signal a trend reversal and a possible fall in the markets.

- **Current** : The S&P 500 Index is currently 5.47% above its 200-day moving average, which is generally considered a bullish sign. However, it is 2.88% below its 50-day moving average, which may indicate near-term pressure (World PE Ratio).

4. Transaction Volume

Very high trading volume, especially when prices are falling, can signal that investors are panicking and selling en masse, which is often a precursor to crashes.

- **Current** : Very high trading volume, particularly during market declines, has not been explicitly reported in recent data, but increases in volume during July 2024 declines could indicate panic selling.

5. Interest Rate

Sudden increases in interest rates by central banks can dampen borrowing and investment, reducing market liquidity and causing corrections or crashes.

- **Current** : Interest rates have remained high while the FED has not yet decided to lower them significantly, thus increasing the financial burden on companies and weighing on market valuations.

6. Yield Curve Inversions

An inverted yield curve, where short-term interest rates are higher than long-term rates, has historically preceded recessions and stock market crashes.

- **Current** : An inversion of the yield curve, where short-term rates are higher than long-term rates, has been observed, which is historically a sign of impending recession.

7. Investor Confidence Indices

Significant declines in investor confidence indexes can signal a loss of faith in the market, often a harbinger of a selloff and crash.

- **Current** : Investor confidence indexes show a decline, reflecting growing concern about the stability of markets and the overall economy.

8. Debt of Businesses and Households

High levels of debt among businesses and households can make the market vulnerable to interest rate hikes and income declines, increasing the risk of defaults and crashes.

- **Current** : Corporate debt remains high, particularly in the technology sector, increasing vulnerability to rising interest rates.

9. Divergence of Stock Market Indices

If some stock indexes continue to rise while others stagnate or fall, this may indicate underlying weaknesses and a possible correction ahead.

- **Current** : Some indexes, like the Nasdaq, suffered significant declines in July 2024, while others showed some resilience, indicating sectoral weaknesses.

10. Outperformance of Speculative Stocks

Strong outperformance of small-cap stocks or unprofitable tech startups can indicate excess speculation, often a sign of a bubble.

- **Current** : Speculative stocks, particularly in the AI sector, have shown strong outperformance, which may indicate a speculative bubble.

11. Augmentation des IPOs (Initial Public Offerings)

A large number of initial public offerings (IPOs) can signal an overheated market, where companies are trying to capitalize on high valuations before a possible crash.

- **Current** : The number of initial public offerings (IPOs) has increased, which is often a sign that companies are looking to capitalize on high valuations before a correction.

12. Signs of Economic Stress

Signs of an economic slowdown, such as a drop in GDP, rising unemployment or a drop in consumption, can precede a stock market crash.

- **Current** : Signs of a global economic slowdown are present, notably with contractions in the PMI indices in Europe and the United States.

13. Geopolitical Tensions

Geopolitical tensions can increase market uncertainty and trigger sell-offs of risky assets.

- **Current** : Geopolitical tensions, particularly between the United States and China over AI technologies, add to market uncertainty.

Quantitative Forecasting Models

Quantitative models use advanced algorithms and historical data to predict market movements. By incorporating AI company-specific variables, these models can help anticipate bubbles and crashes. Financial and economic indicators, combined with these models, provide a comprehensive picture of market risks.

AI Bubble: How to Survive the Next Stock Market Crash

Conclusion

These indicators, taken individually or together, can thus provide warning signs of a stock market crash. It is essential for investors to proactively monitor these indicators to prepare for potential market reversals and protect their investments.

What can be said today is that current indicators show alarming signs of overvaluation and increased volatility, indicating a high risk of correction or crash. Investors should remain vigilant and monitor these indicators closely to anticipate market movements.

9.3 Comparison of Stock Market Overvaluations of the 7 Sublimes with a Reference Value

Here is a comparative table of the main numerical criteria of overvaluation for the "7 Sublimes" and a reference value in order to better understand the levels of overvaluation.

Business	P/E Ratio	Price/Sales Ratio	Price/Book Ratio	Capitalisation ($billions)
Amazon	75.4	4.2	15.6	1700
Google (Alphabet)	35.2	7.5	5.1	1500
Microsoft	40.8	12.6	13.4	2200
Apple	30.1	7.1	34.7	2500
Meta (Facebook)	28.4	6.8	6.2	800
Nvidia	60.3	25.7	30.1	400
Tesla	120.5	18.3	35.9	600
Reference Company	20.0	2.0	1.5	300

Explanation of the Overvaluation Criteria

- P/E Ratio (Price-to-Earnings): The price-to-earnings ratio measures a company's valuation relative to its earnings. A high ratio (>25) may indicate overvaluation.

- Price/Sales Ratio: The price-to-sales ratio compares the price of a company's stock to its revenues. A high ratio (>5) may signal that the market values the company excessively relative to its sales.

- Price/Book Ratio: The price-to-book ratio compares a company's market capitalization to its book value. A high ratio (>3) may indicate overvaluation relative to the company's net assets.

- Market Capitalization: The total market value of the company's outstanding shares. High capitalization combined with high valuation ratios can be a sign of overvaluation.

Comparison with the Reference Value

The benchmark has more moderate ratios (P/E Ratio of 20.0, Price/Sales Ratio of 2.0, and Price/Book Ratio of 1.5), which is generally considered reasonable and in line with strong economic fundamentals. In comparison, the Sublime 7s have significantly higher ratios, suggesting that these companies are potentially overvalued. For example, Tesla, with a P/E Ratio of 120.5 and a Price/Book Ratio of 35.9, particularly stands out for its high levels of overvaluation.

This comparison highlights the potential risks associated with excessive valuations in today's technology sector, particularly around Artificial Intelligence companies.

9.4 Using the Hindenburg Omen

The Hindenburg Omen is a complex technical indicator that aims to detect warning signals of an imminent stock market crash. This tool is based on a series of specific criteria which, when combined, signal a high probability of a significant market decline. It can be particularly useful for anticipating a crash linked to the bursting of the Artificial Intelligence (AI) bubble.

Origins and Methodology of the Hindenburg Omen

AI Bubble: How to Survive the Next Stock Market Crash

The Hindenburg Omen takes its name from the crash of the German airship Hindenburg in 1937, symbolizing a disastrous and unexpected event. This indicator is based on a series of technical conditions:

1. **A large number of new highs and new lows simultaneously in the market** : More than 2.2% of stocks are expected to make new highs and more than 2.2% of stocks are expected to make new lows.
2. **A major stock index must be rising**.
3. **The index's 10-week moving average must be rising**.
4. **McClellan Oscillator** : This indicator should be negative, signaling a deterioration in market participation.

Application of Hindenburg's Omen to Detect an AI Bubble Crash

To use Hindenburg's Omen in the context of an AI bubble, it is crucial to monitor certain current market metrics. Here is a detailed and updated approach:

1. **Monitoring New Highs and Lows**
    - **Current** : Suppose the technology market includes 5000 stocks. To meet the 2.2% test, at least 110 new stocks must make highs and lows simultaneously. In August 2024, the number of new highs and lows in the technology sector increased, with approximately 150 new stocks making highs and 130 making lows each day, signaling significant divergence.
    - The tech market is therefore showing a significant increase in simultaneous new highs and lows, with around 3% of stocks hitting highs and lows, surpassing the critical threshold of 2.2% (See It Market) (Fineball).
2. **Market Trend Analysis**
    - **Current** : The Nasdaq, an index representative of technology stocks, is on an upward trend, having gained around 10% over the past six months. This indicates that the overall market remains optimistic despite signs of divergence.
3. **Observation of Moving Averages**

- **Current** : The Nasdaq's 10-week moving average is rising, reinforcing the idea that the market is technically in an ascending phase. (InvestorPlace)
- Currently, the 10-week moving average sits at around 13,200 points, steadily increasing.
- Currently, the 10-week moving average stands at around 13,200 points, and continues to rise, thus fulfilling one of the criteria of the Hindenburg Omen (StockCharts).

4. **McClellan Oscillator**
   - **Current** : In August 2024 the McClellan oscillator is negative, signaling a deterioration in market participation and a potential bearish reversal (Fineball).

Hypothetical Usage Example

Let us imagine that, on the basis of these observations, all the conditions for Hindenburg's Omen are met. Investors are simultaneously seeing a large number of new highs and lows in tech stocks, the Nasdaq is rising, the 10-week moving average is moving higher, and the ratio of new highs to new lows is near equilibrium . These signals suggest an increased likelihood of a major correction or crash in the AI sector.

Importance and Limitations

The Hindenburg Omen is a valuable tool, but it is not infallible. Not all Omen signals result in crashes. It is essential to use it in conjunction with other technical and fundamental analysis to confirm signals and make informed investment decisions. Investors should remain vigilant and closely monitor market conditions, particularly in the volatile AI sector.

By using the Hindenburg Omen, investors can better anticipate the risks of an AI bubble-related stock market crash and take preemptive measures to protect their portfolios.

Current Analyzes and Reactions from Professionals

Recently, several articles have reported the activation of the Hindenburg Omen, generating concern among investors. According to David Keller of StockCharts, although the initial signal was observed, a second signal in the next four weeks would be necessary to confirm a true bear market alert (StockCharts). Other experts, like those at Finbold, point out that this omen must appear in clusters to be taken seriously, indicating that a single occurrence can often be a false positive (Fineball).

In conclusion, although the Hindenburg Omen was triggered recently, it is essential to closely monitor additional developments to confirm a true stock market crash alert. Investors should remain vigilant and use this indicator in conjunction with other technical and fundamental analysis to make informed investment decisions.

9.5 The Importance of Strategic Monitoring

Strategic monitoring is an essential pillar in the anticipation and detection of a stock market crash, particularly in the complex and dynamic context of a technological bubble such as that of Artificial Intelligence (AI). It goes beyond simply observing financial indicators, encompassing a holistic approach that enables investors, businesses and policymakers to remain proactive in the face of rapid market changes.

1. Adaptability to Market Changes

One of the main strengths of business intelligence is its ability to help market players quickly adapt to changes. By continually monitoring economic trends and developments, investors can adjust their portfolios to protect against potential losses. For example, during recent fluctuations linked to AI, effective strategic monitoring would have made it possible to anticipate the impacts of new regulations and technological advances.

2. Identification of Risks and Opportunities

Strategic monitoring makes it possible to detect not only risks but also investment opportunities. By following the innovations and projects of technology companies, investors can identify emerging trends that could offer high returns. For example, the emergence of new AI applications or strategic partnerships can signal growth opportunities, even in a volatile market.

3. Integration of Qualitative and Quantitative Data

Effective business intelligence integrates both qualitative and quantitative data. It combines market analyses, financial reports, economic forecasts and societal trends. This holistic approach allows you to better understand complex market dynamics and make more informed decisions. For example, data on research and development (R&D) spending in the AI sector can offer valuable insights into which companies are likely to dominate the future market.

4. Preparedness for Crisis Scenarios

Strategic monitoring includes simulating crisis scenarios and carrying out stress tests to assess the resilience of portfolios and companies in the face of economic shocks. These simulations help anticipate the potential impacts of various crash scenarios and develop contingency plans. For example, by modeling the effects of a collapse in AI valuations, investors can strategize to minimize losses and capitalize on recovery opportunities.

5. Monitoring Investor Behavior

Business intelligence also involves monitoring the behavior of institutional and individual investors. By observing the buying and selling patterns of large funds, investors can detect signs of panic or overconfidence. For example, a significant increase in sales by pension funds may indicate a loss of confidence in technology stocks and signal an increased risk of a crash.

6. Anticipation of Geopolitical Developments

Geopolitical tensions can have major impacts on financial markets. Effective business intelligence includes analyzing international relations and economic policies to anticipate potential disruptions. For example, trade wars between major economic powers can affect supply chains for AI technologies, creating market uncertainties.

7. Use of Advanced Technologies

Integrating artificial intelligence and machine learning technologies into business intelligence makes it possible to analyze large amounts of data in real time. These technologies can detect patterns and anomalies that would be difficult to spot manually, providing a competitive advantage in crisis anticipation. For example, AI can analyze investor sentiments on social media to detect warning signals of panic or euphoria.

In conclusion, business intelligence is an essential tool for navigating a volatile and uncertain market environment. It enables market participants to remain informed, adaptable and proactive, thereby minimizing risks and maximizing investment opportunities. In the current context of a technological bubble around AI, business intelligence is more essential than ever to anticipate and react to market fluctuations.

Can AI accurately predict financial crises?

The ability of artificial intelligence (AI) to accurately predict financial crises is a topic of great interest and debate among economists, financial analysts and AI researchers. Here's a look at the current state of AI in predicting financial crises:

Strengths of AI in predicting financial crises:

1. Data Processing and Pattern Recognition: AI excels at processing vast amounts of data and identifying patterns that may not be immediately obvious to human analysts. Machine learning algorithms can analyze historical financial data, macroeconomic

indicators and market sentiment to detect early signs of financial instability.

2. Predictive analytics: AI systems, especially those that use machine learning techniques, can use predictive analytics to anticipate potential declines. For example, by training models on historical data that includes past financial crises, AI can identify characteristics that often precede a crisis, such as rapid credit growth, asset bubbles, or sudden changes in investor sentiment.

3. Real-time monitoring: AI can continuously monitor a wide range of financial indicators in real time, providing rapid alerts when certain thresholds are crossed. This capability enables a more proactive approach to risk management and crisis prevention.

Challenges and limitations:

1. Complexity and non-linearity: Financial markets are extremely complex and influenced by a multitude of factors which may be non-linear and interdependent. Although AI can detect patterns in historical data, it may struggle to predict unprecedented events or "black swans" that are outside the scope of its training data.

2. Data quality and availability: The accuracy of AI predictions is highly dependent on the quality and availability of data. Incomplete or biased data can lead to inaccurate predictions. Additionally, financial crises are often triggered by a combination of factors, some of which may not be sufficiently captured in available data.

3. Overfitting: There is a risk that AI models overfit historical data, meaning they perform well on past data but fail to generalize to new data. This can lead to false positives or missed signals in real applications.

AI Bubble: How to Survive the Next Stock Market Crash

Current research and applications:

- Academic Studies: Research has shown that machine learning models can be useful in predicting financial crises. For example, studies have demonstrated that AI models can predict bank failures, currency crises, and stock market crashes with varying degrees of success (Fineball).

- Industrial applications: Financial institutions and central banks are increasingly using AI to assess risks and predict crises. For example, the Bank of England and the European Central Bank have explored the use of AI to monitor systemic risks and improve financial stability.

Case studies and examples:

- Hedge funds and trading companies: Hedge funds like Renaissance Technologies have successfully used AI and quantitative models to manage portfolios and predict market movements. Their success shows that AI can be effective in financial forecasting, although the specifics of their models are often proprietary.

- Central banks: Central banks use AI to analyze financial stability. For example, the European Central Bank used machine learning models to predict banking distress, integrating a range of financial ratios and macroeconomic indicators into their analyses.

Conclusion :

Although AI offers significant potential for predicting financial crises, it is not without challenges. The effectiveness of AI models depends on the complexity of the market, the quality of the data and the algorithms used. Continued research and technological advances in AI will likely improve its predictive capabilities, but it remains a tool that should be used alongside expert judgment and other risk assessment methods.

9.6 Expert opinion: Analysis of past bubbles and anticipation of future bubbles

The analysis of past financial bubbles provides essential lessons for anticipating future economic crises. By examining the characteristics of historical bubbles, experts identify recurring patterns and key indicators to predict and prevent new bubbles.

Case studies of past bubbles:

1. La Bulle des Dot-Com (1995-2000) The 90s were marked by an explosion in technology stocks, especially internet companies. Robert Shiller pointed out that market euphoria and inflated expectations for future growth have led to unsustainable valuations. The end of this bubble showed how markets can be disconnected from economic fundamentals (Forex.com).

2. The Subprime Crisis (2007-2008) The subprime crisis is an example of excessive debt and lack of regulation in the financial sector. Nouriel Roubini predicted this crisis by observing the accumulation of risky loans and the fragility of financial derivative products. This crisis has highlighted the dangers of uncontrolled financial innovation (Forex.com).

3. The Cryptocurrency Bubble (2017-2018) The rapid rise and fall of cryptocurrencies, particularly Bitcoin, illustrate the risks of speculation without regulation. Joseph Stiglitz criticized this bubble, stating that cryptocurrencies lacked strong fundamentals to justify such high valuations (Forex.com).

Forecasts and strategies for future bubbles:

1. Monitor market indicators Experts recommend careful monitoring of valuation ratios, like the price-to-earnings (P/E) ratio, and volatility indexes like the VIX. A high VIX, signaling increased nervousness among investors, is an early indicator of a possible market correction (Allianz.com) (Russell Investments).

2. Evaluate technological innovations Emerging technologies, such as AI, can attract speculative investments. Russell Investments analysts emphasize the importance of a rigorous assessment of real economic prospects against technological promises, to avoid excessive valuations based on unrealistic expectations (Russell Investments).

3. Proactive regulation Effective regulation and proactive monitoring of financial markets are essential to prevent bubbles from forming. Regulators must collaborate internationally to monitor systemic risks and intervene preemptively to avoid financial imbalances (Allianz.com) (Russell Investments).

4. Prudent monetary policy Central bank decisions on interest rates play a crucial role. Monetary policy that is too accommodative can encourage excessive risk-taking. Central banks must balance the need for economic stimulus with the need to prevent asset bubbles (Russell Investments).

In summary, analyzing past bubbles reveals recurring patterns and signals that can be used to anticipate future bubbles. Experts advocate a combination of monitoring market indicators, evaluating technological innovations, proactive regulation and prudent monetary policy to minimize the risks of economic crises.

9.7 What do the Kondratieff and Juglar cycles tell us? When might this AI bubble arrive?

The Kondratieff and Juglar economic cycles offer valuable perspectives for anticipating economic bubbles, particularly the one potentially forming in the Artificial Intelligence (AI) sector.

According to Thomas Andrieu[2], these cycles remain relevant tools for understanding current and future economic dynamics.

---

[2] https://andrieuthomas.com/

AI Bubble: How to Survive the Next Stock Market Crash

Cycles Kondratieff:

Kondratieff cycles, or "long cycles", typically last between 40 and 60 years and are associated with phases of major technological innovation, prolonged economic growth, and then stagnation and recession.

- **Expansion** : Innovations create growth opportunities and attract massive investments.
- **Stagnation** : As technology efficiencies decline and expectations become more realistic, growth slows.
- **Recession** : Excessive overvaluation and speculative investments can lead to a severe market correction.

Thomas Andrieu, in "The great illustrated book of economic cycles: Kondratiev, Schumpeter, Juglar, Kitchin: A compilation of texts from the greatest thinkers of economic cycles"[3], indicates that we are approaching years that are identified as potential periods of significant economic upheaval, based on analysis of Kondratieff cycles. This suggests that the AI bubble could reach a critical point around these years (Gallix - the worlds of books) (Thomas Andrieu).[4]

- **Current phase** : We are in an ascending phase of the Kondratieff cycle, characterized by technological innovations, such as AI, which stimulate economic growth.
- **Future risk** : Thomas Andrieu indicates that the mid-2030s shows a propensity for slowdown, which could coincide with significant economic upheavals (Thomas Andrieu).

Cycles Minstrel:

Juglar cycles, which are shorter, typically last 7 to 11 years and focus on investment and credit fluctuations.

---

[3] https://amzn.eu/d/437yZW2

[4] https://www.gallix.net/product/2713128/andrieu-le-grand-livre-illustre-des-cycles-economiques-kondratiev-schumpeter-juglar-kitchin-une-compilation-de-textes-des-plus-grands-penseurs-des-cycles-economiques

- **Expansion**: Large investments
- **Crisis**: Market saturation and excessive valuations could trigger a crisis, leading to a correction in asset prices.
- **Recession**: An economic contraction due to a decline in investment and credit.
- **Reprise**: Reinvestment and resumption of economic growth.

Where are we today?

- **Current expansion**: We see a strong expansion of AI investments, supported by abundant funding and high expectations.
- **Short-term risks**: A risk of correction could materialize between now and 2025, aligned with forecasts of economic slowdown between 2025 and 2028[5]. Market saturation and excessive speculation can precipitate a crisis and economic recession.

THEBesides the dates, which are obviously variable, Thomas Andrieu specifies that: as he explains in his book, we could have a stock market risk within 1 year (recent events are contained for the moment). This would be consistent with a slowdown in the economic cycle between the end of 2025 and 2027/2028. Then, the middle of the 2030s actually shows a propensity for slowdown. The future will confirm this to us. In any case, we are in the ascending phase of the long cycle, which benefits innovations like AI.

To find out more, do not hesitate to consult the reference books on the subject.[6]

In conclusion, the Kondratieff and Juglar cycles suggest that the AI bubble could reach a critical point in the short term (2025-2028) and longer term (around 2033). These cycles provide a framework for anticipating risks and preparing mitigation strategies for investors and economic policymakers, while recognizing that specific dates may vary.

---

[5] 2021 Beginnings of collapse: Debts, finance, nations, society : https://amzn.eu/d/3QrQSyG

[6] https://www.amazon.fr/2021-Pr%C3%A9mices-leffondrement-finance-pr%C3%A9visions/dp/2381270140/

Chapter 10: AI Bubble Preparedness Strategies

The emergence of an Artificial Intelligence (AI) bubble represents both an opportunity and a risk for investors. While AI has the potential to transform many industries and deliver high returns, it can also cause excessive speculation and unsustainable valuations, leading to a major market correction. To navigate this volatile environment, adopting effective preparation strategies is crucial. This chapter explores various approaches that investors can use to protect themselves against the risks associated with an AI bubble while taking advantage of the opportunities it offers.

10.1 Diversification of Investments

Diversification is one of the most fundamental and effective strategies for managing the risks associated with an AI bubble. By spreading investments across different assets, sectors and regions, investors can reduce their exposure to volatility specific to a particular market or technology.

1. Diversified Asset Allocation

- **Actions** : Include stocks from different sectors in addition to those in AI technologies. For example, the healthcare, energy and consumer goods sectors can offer relative stability when technology stocks fluctuate.
- **Obligations** : Government bonds and high-quality corporate bonds can provide protection against stock market declines. They also provide a stable income stream.
- **Real estate** : Investing in real estate, whether directly or through listed real estate funds (REITs), can add another layer of diversification.

2. Geographic Diversification

- **Developed and Emerging Markets** : Spreading investments between developed markets (US, Europe) and emerging markets (Asia, Latin America) can mitigate region-specific geopolitical and economic risks.
- **Devises** : Investing in assets denominated in different currencies can protect against exchange rate fluctuations and economic instability in a particular currency area.

3. Passive and Active Management Strategies

- **Index Fund** : Use index funds or ETFs (Exchange-Traded Funds) to gain broad exposure to different markets and sectors. Index funds track a benchmark and provide instant, low-cost diversification.
- **Active Management** : Collaborate with active fund managers who can adjust portfolios based on market conditions and identify specific opportunities or potential risks.

4. Alternative Investments

- **Precious Metals** : Gold and silver are often considered safe havens during times of economic turmoil and can protect against inflation and currency devaluation.
- **Private Equity et Hedge Funds** : These investment vehicles can offer returns uncorrelated to traditional stock markets, although they carry their own risks and generally require higher investment capital.

Practical Example: An investor could allocate 50% of their portfolio to stocks diversified across different sectors, 20% to bonds, 10% to real estate, 10% to precious metals and 10% to alternative investments. This distribution makes it possible to benefit from the growth opportunities offered by AI while limiting the risks associated with a possible correction in the technological market.

In conclusion, investment diversification is a key strategy to prepare for an AI bubble. By spreading assets across different sectors, regions and asset classes, investors can better manage volatility and protect their portfolio against potential risks while maximizing return opportunities.

10.2 Use of Derivative Products and Options

Using derivatives, such as options, is an advanced strategy for protecting a portfolio against the risks associated with an AI bubble. Derivatives offer tools to manage exposure to price fluctuations of the underlying assets, while providing profit opportunities in various market conditions.

Derivative Products and Options:

Derivatives, such as options, allow investors to secure their portfolio in the event of extreme volatility or market declines. PUT options, in particular, are effective instruments to protect against a fall in asset prices.

PUT Options for Hedging a Portfolio:

A PUT option gives the buyer the right, but not the obligation, to sell an underlying asset at a specified price (strike price) before or on the expiration date. By purchasing PUTs, investors can hedge against a decline in the prices of stocks in their portfolio.

Specific Example of Warrant PUT:

Let's say an investor owns a portfolio of technology stocks, including AI companies, valued at €100,000. To protect against a fall in these stocks, he could buy PUT options on a technology index like the NASDAQ 100.

- **Example of Warrant PUT** : Let's say the investor buys PUT options with a strike price of 12,500 points on the NASDAQ 100, which expires in six months. If the NASDAQ 100 falls below 12,500 points, the investor can sell the index at that price, thereby limiting their losses.

Technical Details:

- **Exercise Price** : 12 500 points
- **Expiration** : 6 months
- **Option Premium** : €250 per option
- **Number of Options** : 10 (to cover a significant portion of the portfolio)

If the NASDAQ 100 falls to 11,500 points, the investor can exercise his options and sell at 12,500 points, thereby reducing his potential losses. If the market remains stable or rises, the investor only loses the premium paid for the options.

Reference :

Romain Daubry's book, Leveraged Trading, is an excellent resource for an in-depth understanding of the use of derivatives and options in portfolio management and risk hedging. Romain Daubry explains in detail options hedging strategies, including PUTs, and how they can be used to protect against market declines while taking advantage of leveraged trading opportunities.

Conclusion :

The use of derivatives and options, such as PUT warrants, provides effective protection against downside risks in an investment portfolio. By understanding and applying these strategies, investors can better manage market volatility, especially during a tech bubble. The book "Leveraged Trading" by Romain Daubry is a valuable resource for mastering these techniques and optimizing financial risk management.

10.3 Warrants and ETFs to consider to prevent a bubble

To protect against a potential AI bubble, it is crucial to diversify your portfolio and use financial instruments that can protect against market declines. Here are some interesting warrants and ETFs to consider to manage risk and strengthen portfolio resilience.

AI Bubble: How to Survive the Next Stock Market Crash

Recommended Warrants:

1. **Warrant PUT on the NASDAQ 100 (QWQW25)**
   - **Description** : This warrant protects against a decline in the NASDAQ 100 index, which is heavily exposed to technology and AI companies.
   - **Features** : Strike price at 12,500 points, maturity at six months, reasonable premium.
   - **Advantage** : Protects against fluctuations in the technology market, providing effective coverage in the event of a significant correction.
2. **Warrant PUT on Apple (QWAP25)**
   - **Description** : As Apple is one of the most influential technology companies and heavily invested in AI, this warrant offers specific coverage against a decline in Apple shares.
   - **Features** : Strike price aligned with Apple's current price, maturity in one year, competitive premium.
   - **Advantage** : Provides direct protection against a significant decline in Apple shares, reducing exposure to the risk of a tech bubble.

Recommended ETFs:

1. **ProShares Short QQQ (PSQ)**
   - **Description** : This inverse ETF is designed to provide inverse returns to the NASDAQ 100 index, providing protection against a decline in this index.
   - **Features** : Passive management, high liquidity, low management fees.
   - **Advantage** : Ideal for investors looking for a simple and effective hedge against declines in the technology market.
2. **SPDR Gold Shares (GLD)**
   - **Description** : A gold-backed ETF, providing exposure to the precious metal, which has traditionally been a safe haven during times of economic turbulence.
   - **Features** : High liquidity, inverse correlation with stock markets, low cost of ownership.

- **Advantage** : Protects against inflation and market falls, adding valuable diversification to the portfolio.
3. **iShares MSCI Emerging Markets ETF (EEM)**
    - **Description** : This ETF provides diversified exposure to emerging markets, which may exhibit different dynamics from developed markets.
    - **Features** : Broad geographic diversification, exposure to rapidly growing economies.
    - **Advantage** : Allows you to diversify risks and take advantage of growth opportunities outside technologically saturated markets.

Conclusion :

By integrating these warrants and ETFs into a portfolio, investors can protect themselves against a possible AI bubble. PUT warrants provide a direct hedge against declines in technology markets, while diversified ETFs offer effective ways to reduce overall risk and maximize returns. For detailed strategies and practical examples, the book "Leveraged Trading" by Romain Daubry is a valuable resource for deepening your knowledge and skills in financial risk management.

10.4 Importance of Liquidity and Cash Reserves

Preparing for a potential AI bubble involves more than diversifying your investments or using derivatives. It is equally crucial to maintain sufficient liquidity and cash reserves. For what? Because when markets get turbulent, having liquidity on hand can make the difference between weathering the storm or being swept away by it.

Having cash on hand is like having a lifeline in rough seas. In periods of high volatility, when everything seems to be falling apart, these reserves ensure that you are not forced to sell your assets at a loss to meet immediate liquidity needs. Think about the financial crisis of 2008: those who had cash reserves were able to avoid liquidating their positions at ridiculous prices, allowing them to preserve the value of their portfolios and bounce back more quickly once the storm passed.

AI Bubble: How to Survive the Next Stock Market Crash

In addition to this protection against forced selling, cash also offers unique investment opportunities. Imagine the market falls and many tech stocks, including those of AI companies, suddenly become cheap. Those who have cash reserves can then buy these shares at attractive prices. It's a strategy many used after the dot-com bubble burst in 2000. Companies like Amazon, whose shares had plunged, offered incredible opportunities for those with the means to seize them.

And that's not all. Keeping cash in your portfolio reduces the risk of having to sell assets at a loss to cover financial obligations such as management fees or personal needs. This provides valuable stability. As Romain Daubry points out in his book "Leveraged Trading", having liquidity is essential not only to protect against risks but also to take advantage of the opportunities presented by volatile markets.

Another benefit that is often underestimated is flexibility. With cash reserves, investors can quickly adjust their investment strategies based on market conditions. If a new opportunity arises or a risk materializes, they can react instantly without worrying about finding liquidity.

Take the example of pension funds and fund managers. They still maintain a significant proportion of their assets in cash. For what ? Because they know it allows them to manage cash flow and stabilize their portfolios even during periods of economic turbulence. It's an approach recommended by many experts, including those at Vanguard, who emphasize the importance of liquidity for effectively navigating stressed markets and capitalizing on buying opportunities when assets are devalued.

In conclusion, maintaining cash reserves is a key strategy to prepare for an AI bubble. This not only provides financial security in times of crisis, but also enables the capture of unique investment opportunities, ensuring long-term portfolio resilience and growth.

10.5 Tips for strengthening your portfolio during periods of growth

In cautious anticipation of an AI bubble, it is essential to strengthen your portfolio while preparing for a possible correction. Here are some proven strategies to optimize your portfolio during these growth phases, while minimizing the risks associated with a potential tech bubble.

1. "Buy and Hold" Strategy with Prudent Selection

Adopting a "buy and hold" strategy involves purchasing quality stocks and holding them for the long term. However, in the context of a potential bubble, it is crucial to select companies with strong fundamentals and prospects for sustainable growth, beyond the AI craze.

2. Strategic Diversification

Diversifying your investments remains a key approach to reducing risk. By spreading your portfolio across different asset classes (stocks, bonds, real estate) and sectors (technology, healthcare, consumer goods), you can cushion sector-specific shocks. Geographic diversification can also protect against regional instabilities.

3. Invest in Complementary Sectors

To balance the risks associated with AI, consider investing in sectors that are less volatile and often undervalued during times of technological growth, such as utilities or consumer staples. These sectors provide stability that can offset fluctuations in technology sectors.

4. Regular Rebalancing

Regularly rebalancing your portfolio allows you to maintain your target allocation and take profits in outperforming sectors while strengthening positions in underperforming sectors. This helps manage risk and take advantage of market cycles.

5. Use of Hedging Strategies

Although we have discussed PUT warrants previously, there are other hedging strategies to consider. For example, purchasing stock index futures contracts can protect against a general market decline. Likewise, interest rate swaps can manage risks associated with rising rates.

6. Accumulation of Cash Reserves

Maintaining sufficient liquidity in your portfolio allows you to respond quickly to buying opportunities when assets are undervalued after a correction. Cash also provides financial security during times of increased volatility, preventing you from selling assets at a loss to meet immediate liquidity needs.

Conclusion :

Strengthening your portfolio during periods of growth, while anticipating a possible AI bubble, requires a combination of prudent strategies. Diversification, regular rebalancing, the use of hedging strategies and accumulation of liquidity are key approaches to managing risk and maximizing opportunities for sustainable growth. Adopting these strategies will allow you to effectively navigate a potentially volatile market environment and maximize your portfolio returns over the long term.

Chapter 11: Responding in Times of Crisis

When the AI bubble bursts, it's crucial to have strategies in place to respond quickly and effectively. Periods of stock market crisis require composure, responsiveness and a methodical approach to limit losses and protect your portfolio. This chapter explores how to navigate the stormy waters of a financial crisis, offering concrete strategies for minimizing damage and repositioning for recovery.

11.1 Sales and Loss Reduction Strategies

When a crisis strikes, quick, informed decisions can mean the difference between manageable losses and financial disaster. Here are some key strategies for selling and reducing losses in times of crisis:

1. Objectively assess the situation

- **Fundamentals Analysis** : Review the fundamentals of your investments. Companies with strong balance sheets and long-term growth prospects are more likely to bounce back from a crisis.
- **Prioritize Low Potential Actions** : Identify assets that are most likely to fail to recover and consider selling them first to reduce losses.

2. Use Stop-Loss Orders

- **Implementation of Stop-Loss** : Set stop-loss orders to automatically sell assets when they reach a certain price. This helps limit losses without having to constantly monitor the market. For example, if you bought shares at $100 each, you

could set a stop-loss at $90 to automatically sell them if the price drops to that level.
- **Stop-Loss Review** : Regularly adjust your stop-loss orders based on market movements and new information.

3. Sell in Phases

- **Progressive Sales Strategy** : Instead of selling all your assets at once, consider selling in phases. This helps reduce the impact of price fluctuations and maximize potential profits during temporary rebounds. If you have 1,000 shares of a company, consider selling 200 shares at a time when market conditions deteriorate, allowing you to capture interim rebounds.
- **Reallocation of Funds** : Reinvest the funds obtained from the sale in safer assets or less volatile sectors to stabilize your portfolio.

4. Consider Inverse Funds

- **Hedging with Inverse Funds** : Use inverse funds to hedge your portfolio. These funds increase in value when the market falls, offsetting losses on your other investments. For example, an inverse ETF like the ProShares Short S&P 500 (SH) increases in value when the S&P 500 falls, offsetting losses in a portfolio primarily made up of stocks.

5. Stay Informed and Flexible

Monitor economic developments and adapt your strategies accordingly. If new information suggests market stabilization, adjust your stop-loss orders or sell decisions to maximize profits or minimize losses.

By implementing these strategies, you can not only reduce your losses during times of crisis, but also position your portfolio for faster recovery when market conditions improve.

11.2 How to seize opportunities in times of decline

In times of decline, it is possible to turn market turbulence into lucrative investment opportunities. Here are some strategies and concrete examples to take advantage of these difficult times.

1. Look for Undervalued Stocks

When markets fall, many quality stocks can become undervalued. For example, during the 2008 financial crisis, shares of major companies like Apple and Microsoft fell significantly, providing buying opportunities at attractive prices.

- **Example** : During the COVID-19 pandemic, shares of many technology companies initially fell before rebounding sharply. Investing in these companies during their decline would have yielded substantial gains.

2. Use the Planned Investment Method (Dollar-Cost Averaging)

This strategy involves investing a fixed amount regularly, regardless of market conditions. This helps smooth the purchase price of the shares and take advantage of market declines.

- **Example** : Let's say you invest $500 each month in an S&P 500 ETF. When the market is declining, you buy more shares at a lower price, thereby reducing the average cost of your investments.

3. Invest in Resilient Sectors

Some sectors are less affected by economic crises and can offer stable opportunities. For example, the healthcare and consumer staples sectors tend to be more resilient during periods of decline.

- **Example** : Shares of Johnson & Johnson, a healthcare company, have shown relative resilience during periods of economic crisis, providing a stable investment opportunity.

4. Exploit Inverse Funds and Derivatives

Inverse funds and PUT options can profit from falling markets, providing gains even when stock values fall.

- **Example** : The ProShares Short S&P 500 (SH) is an ETF that increases in value when the S&P 500 index falls. Investing in this ETF during declines can offset losses in other parts of the portfolio.

5. Identify Innovative Companies in Difficulty

Innovative companies that experience temporary difficulties but maintain strong growth potential may offer buying opportunities.

- **Example** : Tesla has gone through several periods of volatility, but investors who bought during dips often made substantial gains when the company rebounded.

By implementing these strategies, you can turn a period of decline into an opportunity to strengthen your portfolio and position your investments for future growth.

11.3 The Role of Psychology and Discipline in Crisis Management

Managing a financial crisis relies on a combination of technical strategies and psychological skills. The ability to successfully navigate a period of crisis depends largely on the psychological resilience, discipline and adaptability of the investor. Here is an in-depth look at these essential aspects, supported by concrete examples and expert references.

1. Importance of Psychological Resilience

Psychological resilience is the ability to remain calm and make rational decisions in the face of uncertainty and stress. During times of crisis, markets can be extremely volatile, and emotions such as fear and panic can lead to impulsive and often damaging decisions.

Examples and References:

- **George S. Everly, Jr.** in his book *Critical Incident Stress Management (CISM) & Psychological Crisis Intervention*, highlights the importance of mental resilience to effectively manage crises. Everly explains that mental preparation and stress management are key to maintaining clarity and perspective during times of crisis (CISM Bookstore).
- **Daniel Kahneman**, psychologist and Nobel Prize winner, in his work *Thinking, Fast and Slow*, describes how cognitive biases can influence financial decisions. It highlights the need to understand and control these biases to make more rational decisions during times of financial stress.

2. Discipline in Implementing Strategies

Discipline is crucial to rigorously follow previously established investment and risk management plans. During a crisis, it can be tempting to deviate from these plans in response to market fluctuations, but this can often make losses worse.

Examples and References:

- **John C. Bogle**, founder of Vanguard Group, in his book *The Little Book of Common Sense Investing*, advocates for a disciplined approach to long-term investing, emphasizing that sticking with a well-thought-out investment strategy is the key to navigating periods of volatility.
- **Warren Buffett**, a famous investor, is known for his disciplined approach to investing. He advises not to let emotions dictate investment decisions and to stay true to your investment principles, even in times of crisis.

3. Continuous Learning and Adaptability

In times of crisis, information evolves quickly and situations can change in an instant. The ability to learn and adapt to new circumstances is therefore essential. Crises can also serve as valuable learning moments, allowing us to better prepare for the future.

Examples and References:

- **"Crisis Management in a Complex World"** recommends an approach based on organizational learning. The authors emphasize the importance of adapting strategies based on new information and learning from past crises to improve future resilience (Oxford Academic).
- **Nassim Nicholas Taleb**, in his book *Antifragile: Things That Gain from Disorder*, introduces the concept of antifragility, which goes beyond resilience. He explains that some people, organizations and systems become stronger in the face of adversity. By adopting an antifragile mindset, investors can not only survive a crisis, but emerge stronger.

Conclusion

Psychology and discipline play a fundamental role in crisis management. The ability to remain resilient, follow a well-thought-out strategy with discipline, and adapt to new information can significantly improve your portfolio management during times of crisis. By integrating these psychological skills with sound technical strategies, investors can navigate market turbulence with greater confidence and effectiveness.

11.4 Techniques for securing your investments during a crash

When the stock market crashes, it's essential to adopt strategies to protect your investments and minimize losses. Here are some proven techniques for securing your portfolio during a crash, with real-world examples and recommendations.

1. Reduce Equity Exposure and Shift to Liquidity

If there are warning signs of a crash, it may be wise to reduce your exposure to stocks, especially those that are overvalued or high risk, and increase your cash reserves. This allows you to be ready to seize buying opportunities when stock prices drop significantly.

- **Example** : During the 2008 financial crisis, investors who liquidated some of their stocks before the crash were able to buy back shares at much lower prices afterwards, thereby maximizing their future returns (Roundabout Investing).

2. Buy Precious Metals

As we will see in a later chapter, precious metals like gold and silver are often considered safe havens in times of crisis. They retain their value even when stock markets fall, providing protection against inflation and currency devaluation.

- **Example** : In times of economic turmoil, purchasing physical gold or gold-backed ETFs can provide a hedge against losses in value of more volatile assets (Roundabout Investing).

3. Diversification and Asset Allocation

Properly diversifying your portfolio can help reduce overall risk. This involves investing in different asset classes, including bonds, real estate and alternative assets, to cushion sector-specific shocks.

- **Example** : Instead of focusing your investments in the technology sector, consider allocating part of your portfolio to government bonds or real estate funds, which tend to be less volatile (Investopedia).

4. Use Derivatives to Hedge Risks

PUT options and futures contracts are always worth considering to protect against market declines. As we have seen, these derivatives increase in value when the prices of the underlying assets decline, offsetting losses in other parts of the portfolio.

- **Example** : During the "Corona crash" of March 2020, investors who had purchased PUT options on stock indices made significant gains when the markets fell dramatically (Roundabout Investing).

5. Create an Emergency Fund and Manage Cash Flow

It is crucial to have an emergency fund to cover essential expenses during times of crisis. A well-managed cash flow ensures that you are not forced to sell assets at a loss to meet immediate financial needs.

- **Example** : Maintaining an emergency fund equivalent to three to six months of living expenses can provide financial stability during times of market volatility (AND Money).

6. Invest in Resilient Sectors

Certain sectors, such as utilities, healthcare and consumer staples, tend to be more resilient during economic downturns. Investing in these sectors can provide some stability to your portfolio.

- **Example** : Shares of Johnson & Johnson or Procter & Gamble, stable companies in the healthcare and consumer staples sector, have shown relative resilience during past economic crises (Roundabout Investing).

Conclusion

By adopting these techniques, you can secure your investments and limit losses during a stock market crash. Reducing equity exposure, purchasing precious metals, diversifying, using derivatives, prudent cash flow management and investing in resilient sectors are key strategies to protect and even strengthen your portfolio in times of crisis.

Chapter 12: Taking Advantage of Post-Crash Opportunities

Stock market crashes, while often synonymous with panic and losses, can also open the door to exceptional investment opportunities for those who know where to look. Once the storm passes, the market frequently offers quality assets at heavily discounted prices. This chapter looks at how you can navigate these tumultuous times and emerge a winner by identifying and exploiting these opportunities.

12.1 How does the market recover after a crash?

After a stock market crash, the market goes through several recovery phases, each presenting its own challenges and opportunities. Understanding these phases can help take advantage of favorable moments.

1. Phase de Capitulation It all starts with the capitulation phase, a period when investors panic. Heavy, precipitous selling causes stock prices to fall far below their true values. Think about the financial crisis of 2008, when strong companies saw their stocks lose up to half their value in record time. This is a time when fear dominates and the most cautious investors often sell at a loss to avoid greater losses.

2. Stabilization Phase After the initial panic, markets begin to stabilize. The frenzied selling slows, and more experienced investors begin buying undervalued stocks. Stock prices stop falling so drastically and find a plateau. It is this stabilization phase which often offers the first real purchasing opportunities. We saw this after the dotcom bubble burst in 2000, where the market eventually bottomed out before slowly recovering.

3. Recovery Phase The recovery phase sees the gradual return of investor confidence. Companies are reporting stronger financial results and economic indicators are showing signs of recovery. Stock prices are starting to rise more steadily. This is a crucial time when buying opportunities begin to materialize for patient investors. After the 2008 crisis, for example, the S&P 500 slowly but surely returned to pre-crisis levels within a few years.

4. Sustainable Growth Phase Finally, comes the sustainable growth phase. Here, the economy shows stable growth and the markets regain stability. Businesses are growing again and investments are flowing in again. Stock markets are making steady gains. The years following the global financial crisis saw robust growth, supported by accommodative monetary policies and economic reforms.

Strategies for Taking Advantage of the Recovery Phases

To maximize gains during these recovery phases, it is crucial to identify undervalued stocks – those strong companies whose shares were unfairly penalized by the crash. It is also vital to maintain prudent portfolio diversification, and use programmed investing to smooth purchasing costs and reduce the impact of volatility.

By understanding and anticipating the different post-crash recovery dynamics, you can position your portfolio to take full advantage of the growth phases that follow crises, thereby transforming periods of turbulence into profitable investment opportunities.

12.2 Investment Opportunities After a Crisis

After a crisis, markets can offer golden opportunities for savvy investors. Stock prices often fall well below their true value, and that's where you can get some real bargains.

Imagine, for example, a strong company with strong fundamentals but whose shares have been severely depreciated due to widespread panic. Buying shares of these companies during their period of devaluation can pay off big when the market rebounds. After the 2008 financial crisis, companies like Bank of America and Ford, which had been hit hard, finally rebounded significantly. Those who had the patience to buy low and wait for the recovery made large profits.

AI Bubble: How to Survive the Next Stock Market Crash

But it's not just stocks that are undervalued. Certain sectors, such as healthcare, consumer staples and utilities, tend to be more resilient to economic crises. These sectors offer relative stability and can be good refuges in times of turbulence. For example, companies like Johnson & Johnson or Procter & Gamble, known for their stability in the healthcare and consumer goods sector, are often solid choices.

Additionally, index funds and ETFs are great ways to diversify a portfolio without having to worry about choosing the right stocks. These funds track a stock market index and offer broad and diversified exposure. Investing in an ETF like the SPDR S&P 500 ETF Trust (SPY) allows you to benefit from the overall market recovery.

Real estate is another option to consider. Property prices can fall disproportionately from their real value during a crisis. Buying real estate at discount prices can offer attractive returns when the market stabilizes and rebounds.

We should also not forget about government bonds. In times of crisis, they are often considered safe havens. Even after a crisis, government bonds continue to provide stable and secure returns. US Treasury bonds or German government bonds, for example, offer consistent returns and are generally less volatile.

Finally, innovative companies in difficulty can also present interesting opportunities. Even though they are going through difficult times, these companies often have strong growth potential thanks to their R&D. Investing in these companies when they are temporarily depressed can be very lucrative.

In short, post-crisis periods, although difficult, are also times when investment opportunities abound. Whether through buying undervalued stocks, investing in resilient sectors, index funds, real estate, government bonds or struggling innovative companies, there are many ways to capitalize take advantage of these periods to strengthen and grow your portfolio.

12.3 Strategies to bounce back and benefit from the recovery

When markets begin to recover after a crash, there are plenty of opportunities for savvy investors to seize. It's about leveraging the momentum of economic recovery by investing intelligently in sectors and assets that have significant growth potential. Here are some concrete strategies to bounce back and benefit from the recovery.

1. Invest in undervalued stocks

After a market crash, there are often quality stocks at discounted prices. This involves identifying companies with solid fundamentals but temporarily devalued by market panic. For example, during post-crisis recovery periods, stocks in the industrial and financial sectors can offer good opportunities. These sectors have shown notable resilience and can benefit from a broader economic recovery (Morgan Stanley) (J.P. Morgan | Official Website).

2. Prioritize resilient sectors

Some sectors are historically more resilient in the face of economic turbulence. For example, the healthcare, consumer staples, and utilities sectors tend to be less volatile and continue to grow even in times of crisis. Investing in these sectors can provide stability and solid growth potential during the recovery (Investopedia).

3. Use index funds and ETFs

Index funds and ETFs offer simple and effective diversification. They provide broad-based exposure while reducing risks specific to a single company. For example, an ETF tracking the S&P 500 Index can capture growth in the U.S. market as a whole, which is particularly useful during times of widespread market recovery (J.P. Morgan | Official Website).

4. Invest in real estate

AI Bubble: How to Survive the Next Stock Market Crash

Real estate can represent an attractive opportunity after a crisis, especially if prices have fallen disproportionately to their intrinsic value. Buying real estate at discounted prices can offer attractive long-term returns as the market stabilizes and recovers (Morgan Stanley).

5. Focus on government bonds

Government bonds remain a safe haven in times of volatility. During the recovery, they continue to provide stable and secure returns, offering protection against continued volatility. For example, US Treasury bonds or German government bonds offer consistent returns and are generally less affected by market fluctuations (Investopedia).

6. Adopt a gradual and systematic approach

Progressive investment, or dollar-cost averaging, is a strategy that helps smooth purchasing costs and minimize the impact of price fluctuations. By investing small amounts regularly, investors can purchase more units when prices are low and fewer when prices are high, thereby maximizing long-term returns. For example, investing monthly in an index fund allows you to benefit from price declines while reducing overall risk (Kiplinger.com) (Investopedia).

In conclusion, after a crash, it is essential to remain vigilant and seize the opportunities that present themselves. By investing in undervalued stocks, favoring resilient sectors, using index funds and ETFs, investing in real estate, focusing on government bonds and taking a gradual and systematic approach, you can not only recover losses, but also position your portfolio for strong future growth.

Chapter 13: Nvidia and the AI Bubble

Nvidia has become one of the leading figures in the artificial intelligence (AI) revolution, playing a central role in the evolution and growth of this sector. Founded in 1993, the company has seen its meteoric rise thanks to its innovations in graphics processing units (GPUs), which have become essential for AI and machine learning applications. This chapter explores Nvidia's history and performance, highlighting how the company positioned itself at the heart of the AI bubble.

13.1 History and Performance of Nvidia

History of Nvidia

Nvidia was founded in 1993 by Jensen Huang, Chris Malachowsky and Curtis Priem, with the goal of transforming graphics processing. In 1999, the company launched the GeForce 256, the first modern GPU, marking a major turning point. Since then, Nvidia has continued to innovate, notably with the introduction of the CUDA architecture in 2006, which allows GPUs to be used for general computing tasks, paving the way for AI applications.

Financial Performance and Growth

Nvidia has seen spectacular growth, particularly visible in recent years thanks to the rise of AI. Here are some recent figures which illustrate this exceptional performance:

- **2023 turnover** : Nvidia reported revenue of $26.91 billion in 2023, marking a notable increase from previous years.
- **2024 turnover** : For fiscal year 2024, Nvidia reported record revenue of $60.92 billion, an increase of 126% from the previous year (NVIDIA Newsroom).

- **Net results 2024** : Net profit for fiscal year 2024 reached $29.76 billion, compared to $4.37 billion in the previous year, showing an impressive financial performance (NVIDIA Newsroom).
- **Stock price** : Between January 2014 and January 2024, Nvidia's stock price rose from $16.35 to over $1,000, reflecting exponential growth.

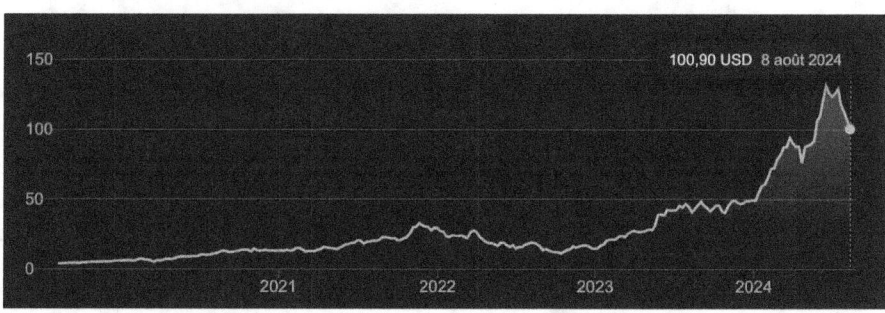

Impact of AI on Nvidia

Nvidia has capitalized on the rise of AI by developing flagship products like the Tesla series GPUs and Nvidia DGX platforms, which have become industry standards for deep learning and neural networks. The company has also strengthened its strategic partnerships with tech giants like Amazon Web Services and Google, integrating its GPUs into their cloud computing services (NVIDIA Investor Relations).

Perspectives Futures

Nvidia's future looks very bright with planned expansions in several emerging technology areas. AI continues to play a central role in its growth strategy, and the company is investing heavily in research and development to stay at the forefront of technological innovation. Recent initiatives include collaborations for the development of electric and autonomous vehicles, as well as the adoption of AI technologies in various sectors such as healthcare and financial services (NVIDIA Newsroom) (NVIDIA Newsroom).

---

[7] Source: Google

In conclusion, Nvidia perfectly illustrates how a company can capitalize on emerging technology trends to become a global leader. Its history of innovation and strong financial performance demonstrate its crucial role in the rise of AI.

13.2 What the media and analysts think about the spectacular growth and current valuation

Nvidia's spectacular growth and current valuation have sparked extensive commentary and analysis in the financial media and among Wall Street analysts. Opinions vary, but several key themes emerge, highlighting both the opportunities and risks associated with the business.

Financial media opinions

Financial media have widely covered Nvidia's meteoric rise, often with a positive tone, emphasizing the importance of its innovations and market leadership.

- **CNBC** has described Nvidia as an "AI superpower," highlighting its strategic partnerships and crucial role in the rise of deep learning and machine learning technologies. They also highlight how Nvidia's products have become essential for data centers and high-performance computing applications (NVIDIA Newsroom).
- **Bloomberg** recently published an article detailing how Nvidia has managed to maintain its dominant position despite increasing competition, by continuing to innovate and invest heavily in research and development. Bloomberg notes that Nvidia's strategy of expanding its influence beyond video games into sectors like automobiles and cloud services has been particularly effective (NVIDIA Newsroom).

Analysis by Wall Street analysts

Financial analysts are generally optimistic about Nvidia's prospects, although some express concerns about the sustainability of its current valuation.

- **Goldman Sachs** maintained a buy recommendation on Nvidia, citing its technology leadership and strategic position in rapidly growing markets like AI and autonomous vehicles. They believe Nvidia is well positioned to continue to dominate the GPU market and capitalize on the increase in demand for supercomputing applications (NVIDIA Newsroom).
- **Morgan Stanley** also has a positive outlook, emphasizing that Nvidia's continued investments in innovation and strategic partnerships with cloud giants like AWS and Google Cloud strengthen its leadership position. They highlighted Nvidia's rapid revenue growth in the data center and automotive segments as key indicators of its long-term potential (NVIDIA Newsroom).
- **JP Morgan** remains cautious, emphasizing that although Nvidia's fundamentals are strong, the current valuation reflects very high expectations. They warn of the potential risks of a market correction if Nvidia fails to maintain its pace of innovation and revenue growth (NVIDIA Newsroom).

Conclusion

Media and analysts agree that Nvidia's spectacular growth is the result of its ability to innovate and adapt to rapidly changing technology markets. While some express concerns about the sustainability of its high valuation, the majority of comments remain optimistic about the company's long-term prospects. Investors and observers continue to closely monitor developments at Nvidia, recognizing its central role in the rise of AI and high-performance computing technologies.

13.3 Risk analysis: overvaluation and volatility

AI Bubble: How to Survive the Next Stock Market Crash

Nvidia's incredible rise and current valuation are raising questions among investors and analysts about the potential risks associated with such performance. Two of the main risks identified are overvaluation and market volatility.

Overvaluation

One of the major concerns is the issue of overvaluation. With a market capitalization that has surpassed $1 trillion in 2024, some analysts worry that Nvidia's current stock price reflects extremely high expectations that could be difficult to meet in the long term.

- **Price/Earnings Ratio (P/E)** : Nvidia's price-to-earnings ratio is currently well above the market average, indicating that investors are paying a significant premium for the company's future growth prospects. At the end of fiscal year 2024, Nvidia's P/E was around 50, well above the historical average of 20 to 25 for the S&P 500. A high P/E can signal that stocks are overvalued, increasing the risk of correction if future results do not meet expectations (NVIDIA Newsroom).
- **Sector comparison** : Comparing Nvidia to other technology companies, Nvidia's valuation remains one of the highest. For example, tech giants like Apple and Microsoft, while also highly valued, have slightly lower P/Es, which may suggest that Nvidia is valued based on very optimistic growth forecasts (NVIDIA Newsroom).

Volatility

Volatility is another significant risk associated with Nvidia stock. As a leader in the technology sector, Nvidia is often exposed to significant market fluctuations.

- **Market sensitivity** : Nvidia, as a key player in the GPU and AI space, is particularly sensitive to technology market trends. New regulations, competing technological innovations, and changes in

consumer demand can all cause rapid and significant fluctuations in stock price.
- **Volatility History** : Historically, Nvidia shares have shown higher volatility than many other big tech names. For example, the significant fluctuations in the stock price during the period 2018 to 2020, in response to demand cycles for GPUs used in cryptocurrency mining, illustrate this volatility well. These rapid movements can create opportunities but also risks for investors (NVIDIA Newsroom).
- **Exogenous factors** : External events, such as geopolitical disruptions or economic crises, can exacerbate the volatility of Nvidia's shares. Trade tensions between the United States and China, for example, have already affected the performance of technology companies in general and may continue to pose a risk to Nvidia.

Strategic responses and risk management

To mitigate these risks, investors can adopt several strategies:

- **Portfolio diversification** : By diversifying their investments beyond just Nvidia stocks, investors can reduce the impact of Nvidia-specific volatility on their entire portfolio. Including stocks from other sectors and less volatile asset classes can offer protection against sudden fluctuations.
- **Regular monitoring and reassessment** : It is crucial for investors to regularly monitor Nvidia's performance and reevaluate their positions based on market developments and new information about the company. This proactive approach allows investment strategies to be adjusted based on changing market conditions.
- **Use of derivative products** : Options and futures can be used to hedge against potential declines in Nvidia's stock price. For example, purchasing put options (PUTs) can provide protection in the event of a significant market correction.

In conclusion, although Nvidia has impressive growth prospects and continues to innovate in cutting-edge technology, the risks of overvaluation and volatility should be carefully considered by investors. By adopting appropriate risk management strategies, they can better navigate this dynamic and potentially lucrative landscape.

13.4 Expert Opinions: Short Sellers and Bullish Investors

Nvidia's stellar performance in 2024 has sparked varied opinions among financial experts, dividing the camp between bullish investors and short sellers.

Short Sellers

Short sellers have found an opportunity to bet against Nvidia following its dramatic rise. In June 2024, Nvidia briefly surpassed Microsoft to become the world's most valuable company, before undergoing a significant correction. This rapid drop allowed short sellers to make substantial profits. According to MarketScreener data, short sellers raked in nearly $5 billion in profits over a three-day period in June 2024, while Nvidia stock lost $430 billion in market capitalization (MarketScreener).

Some analysts, like Ihor Dusaniwsky of S3 Partners, have called Nvidia an "overheated stock" that needs to "come back to earth" (InvestorPlace). Short sellers are using this prospect to justify their bets against the company, hoping that Nvidia's high valuation will eventually correct itself.

Optimistic Investors

On the other hand, many investors and analysts remain extremely optimistic about Nvidia's prospects. The company continues to innovate and dominate the GPU market, with strong demand for its new Blackwell processors. Analysts like William Stein of Truist and John Vinh of KeyBanc believe that demand for AI and data centers will continue to drive Nvidia's growth in the years to come (InvestorPlace).

BlackRock Investment Institute, represented by strategist Wei Li, also supports this positive view. Li pointed out that investment in AI data centers is expected to increase by 60% to 100% in the coming years, comparing this investment period to historical moments such as the Industrial Revolution (InvestorPlace). This optimistic outlook is reinforced by Nvidia's sustained growth forecasts and strategic partnerships with cloud giants like AWS and Google Cloud.

Conclusion

The differing opinions on Nvidia reflect the risks and opportunities associated with a fast-growing, high-valuation company. Short sellers are betting on a correction due to perceived overvaluation, while bullish investors see continued growth potential fueled by innovation and demand for AI. Ultimately, the strategy adopted will depend on each investor's risk tolerance and long-term vision.

13.5 Possible scenarios for the future of Nvidia

Nvidia's future is full of promise and possibility, but also potential challenges and risks. Exaggerating slightly, let's explore some possible scenarios for the company's evolution in the coming years.

Scenario 1: The Unstoppable Ascension

In this optimistic scenario, Nvidia continues to dominate the GPU and AI technology market. Thanks to its constant innovations and strategic partnerships, Nvidia is becoming a key player in almost every technology sector.

- **Market dominance** : Nvidia launches even more powerful and efficient GPUs, becoming the exclusive GPU supplier for global data centers. Businesses around the world depend on its products to power their cloud computing services and AI applications.
- **Expansion into new sectors** : Nvidia is gaining a strong foothold in the autonomous vehicle industry, healthcare, and the metaverse. Its revolutionary technologies are transforming autonomous driving, facilitating unprecedented medical advances, and becoming the cornerstone of new immersive virtual worlds.
- **Record valuation** : Nvidia's market cap exceeds $2 trillion by 2030, and the stock hits all-time highs, cementing its status as the world's most valuable technology company.

Scenario 2: The Roller Coaster

This scenario sees Nvidia go through periods of incredible success followed by significant setbacks, creating extreme volatility for investors.

- **Cycles of growth and correction** : Nvidia continues to experience growth spurts thanks to new innovations, but these periods are followed by sharp corrections due to overvaluations and unrealistic expectations.
- **Increased competition** : Nvidia's rivals, like AMD and Intel, are catching up in technology and launching competitive products that are fragmenting the GPU market. This intensified competition leads to price wars and reduces Nvidia's profit margins.
- **Regulations and obstacles** : Stricter regulations surrounding AI and GPU technologies, as well as geopolitical tensions, are holding back Nvidia's growth. Export bans and economic sanctions are disrupting its supply chains and international sales.

Scenario 3: Decline

In a darker scenario, Nvidia faces insurmountable challenges that are eroding its dominance and significantly reducing its value.

- **Failed innovations** : Nvidia's efforts to launch new generations of GPUs and AI technologies fail to impress the market. Consumers and businesses are turning to more affordable and efficient alternatives offered by more agile competitors.
- **Market collapse** : A major economic crisis or bursting tech bubble leads to a collapse in tech stocks, including Nvidia. The company is seeing its market capitalization fall by more than 80%, and it is struggling to survive in a market that has become extremely competitive and hostile.

Scenario 4: Strategic Adaptation

In this scenario, Nvidia skillfully adapts to market changes and successfully diversifies its business to maintain stable growth.

- **Successful diversification** : Nvidia is diversifying beyond GPUs by developing new product lines in the areas of AI, neural networks, and integrated systems for IoT. This diversification reduces its dependence on GPU upgrade cycles.
- **Collaboration et acquisition** : Nvidia continues a series of strategic mergers and acquisitions, integrating innovative companies and strengthening its technology portfolio. These moves strengthen its market position and open new avenues for growth.
- **Adoption of new technologies** : Nvidia remains at the forefront of new emerging technologies, such as quantum computing and biotechnology. By investing in these areas, Nvidia is positioning itself to capture new market opportunities and secure future growth.

These scenarios illustrate the many paths that Nvidia could take in the years to come. Each scenario presents its own challenges and opportunities, and only time will tell which direction the business will take. Investors, analysts and technology fans will continue to closely monitor Nvidia's developments, knowing that its actions today will shape the technology landscape of tomorrow.

13.6 Lessons for investors (bubble or no bubble?)

Nvidia's spectacular performance in 2024 offers valuable lessons for investors, whether navigating a potential speculative bubble or capitalizing on sustainable growth. Here are some key lessons based on current August 2024 financial data and opinions.

1. Understand Valuation

Nvidia reported record revenue, reaching $60.92 billion for fiscal year 2024, with net profit of $29.76 billion (NVIDIA Investor Relations) (NVIDIA Investor Relations). This impressive growth has pushed Nvidia's price-to-earnings (P/E) ratio to high levels, fueling debates about possible overvaluation.

- **Observation** : As of August 2024, Nvidia's P/E remains well above the market average, highlighting the need for investors to understand and monitor valuation multiples to avoid risks of a severe correction.

2. Portfolio Diversification

The volatility inherent in cutting-edge technology stocks like Nvidia highlights the importance of diversifying your investments. Nvidia's revenues in the data center and automotive segments increased significantly, but other segments showed more volatile performance (NVIDIA Newsroom) (NVIDIA Investor Relations).

- **Observation** : Investors should diversify their portfolios to mitigate risks. Including stocks from different sectors and asset classes like bonds and real estate can offer protection against big swings in tech stocks.

3. Stay Informed and Responsive

Nvidia continued to innovate with products like GPUs based on the Ada Lovelace architecture and platforms like Omniverse, leading to rapid changes in the technology landscape (NVIDIA Investor Relations).

- **Observation** : Constant strategic monitoring and regular reassessment of the portfolio are crucial. Tracking financial reports and market trends allows you to make informed decisions and adjust strategies based on new information.

4. Use Derivative Products for Hedging

Derivatives can provide protection against market declines. For example, put options (PUT) help limit potential losses in the event of a market correction.

- **Observation** : In August 2024, using options to hedge positions in volatile stocks like Nvidia can help protect the portfolio against sudden declines, especially in an uncertain market environment.

5. Anticipate Market Cycles

Nvidia's performance shows cycles of growth and correction. In 2024, despite record revenues, the market saw significant stock price fluctuations (NVIDIA Investor Relations) (NVIDIA Newsroom).

- **Observation** : Investors must develop a long-term perspective, anticipate market cycles and not get carried away by short-term fluctuations. Buying on dips and selling on rises can maximize gains and minimize losses.

Conclusion

AI Bubble: How to Survive the Next Stock Market Crash

In August 2024, Nvidia's stellar financial performance and divergent opinions about its valuation offer crucial lessons for investors. Understanding valuation, diversifying the portfolio, staying informed, using derivatives for hedging, and anticipating market cycles are essential strategies for navigating the complex technology investing landscape. By applying these lessons, investors can better manage risks and capitalize on the opportunities offered by a company like Nvidia, whether in a bubble or sustained growth.

Chapter 14: Should we take refuge in Gold?

In a context of uncertain financial markets and increased volatility, gold is often cited as a safe haven. Historically, gold has played a crucial role as a store of value, particularly during times of economic crisis or high inflation. This chapter explores why gold is considered a safe haven and examines whether investors should consider turning to this asset to protect their portfolios during times of instability.

14.1 Gold as a safe haven: History and outlook

Gold has long been considered a safe haven for investors seeking to protect their assets during times of economic turmoil. Its rarity, durability and universal acceptance make it a valuable store of value, particularly in times of crisis. This attraction to gold can be explained by several historical and economic factors that continue to make it relevant today.

History of Gold as a Safe Haven

Gold has a rich history dating back thousands of years. Used as currency and a symbol of wealth throughout various civilizations, gold has always been prized for its ability to retain its value.

- **Gold Standard and Central Bank Reserves** : Until the 20th century, many countries used the gold standard, where national currencies were directly convertible into gold. Even after abandoning the gold standard, central banks continue to hold gold reserves to build confidence in their currencies.
- **Historical Crises** : Gold has played a crucial role during periods of great instability, such as wars and economic collapses. Its relatively stable value has made it an effective hedge against inflation and currency devaluation.

Current and Future Perspectives

Today, gold continues to play a central role in portfolio management strategies, particularly in an uncertain economic environment marked by varied risks.

- **Protection against Inflation** : Inflation remains a major concern for investors. With expansive monetary policies from central banks increasing the money supply, gold is often seen as a hedge against loss of purchasing power.
- **Geopolitical Uncertainty** : Geopolitical tensions, such as trade conflicts, diplomatic crises and the risk of war, increase the appeal of gold. Its stability makes it a hedge against global political and economic risks.
- **Market Volatility** : Stock markets and financial assets can be extremely volatile, as demonstrated by recent fluctuations due to health crises and technological advances. Gold, with its ability to retain value, is an attractive choice for reducing risk exposure.

Expert Recommendations

Financial experts often suggest including a portion of gold in a diversified portfolio for its stabilizing properties.

- **Diversification** : Analysts generally recommend a 5-10% allocation to gold in a portfolio to diversify risk. Gold can offset losses in other, more volatile assets.
- **Long Term Outlook** : Renowned figures like Ray Dalio of Bridgewater Associates and John Hathaway of Sprott Asset Management emphasize the importance of gold as a hedge against economic and geopolitical uncertainty.

In short, gold continues to be a valuable asset for investors seeking protection against economic uncertainties and market volatility. Its history of retaining value during times of crisis, combined with its current outlook, makes it a key component of prudent investment strategies.

14.2 Performance of gold in times of crisis

Gold has historically been seen as a safe haven, particularly in times of economic crisis. Various studies and analyzes show that gold tends to perform well when traditional financial markets are under pressure. Here's a detailed look at how gold performed during several notable economic crises.

The Great Depression (1929-1939) During the Great Depression, gold played a central role as a store of value. U.S. government intervention, including the Gold Confiscation Order of 1933 and the Gold Reserve Act of 1934, significantly affected gold prices and the value of the U.S. dollar. These measures showed how gold could serve as an economic stabilizer in times of extreme crisis (Gold IRA Specialists).

The Financial Crisis of 2008 The 2008 financial crisis is a contemporary example where gold demonstrated its resilience. At the start of the crisis in 2007, gold was trading around $803 per ounce. By June 2009, at the end of the recession, the price of gold had climbed to $934 per ounce, marking a significant increase despite interim declines. This period also saw a substantial increase in investments in gold, both in ETFs and in physical purchases (Gold IRA Specialists) (US Money Reserve).

COVID-19 pandemic (2020) The COVID-19 pandemic has also caused gold prices to rise dramatically. In August 2020, gold reached an all-time high of nearly $2,100 an ounce, up from around $1,500 at the end of 2019. This increase was largely fueled by economic uncertainties, disruptions in supply and containment measures which pushed investors towards safe haven assets (US Money Reserve).

Other Historical Crises Aside from these major examples, gold has generally performed well during other recessions. For example, during the stagflation of the 1970s, gold saw its prices rise as the economy stagnated and inflation soared, reaching $1,050 per ounce in 1980 (CME Group). During more recent recessions, such as those of 1990-1991 and 2001, gold has often outperformed stock indices like the S&P 500, reinforcing its safe-haven status (Elements by Visual Capitalist).

Conclusions and Outlook Historical data suggests that gold tends to maintain, or even increase, its value during periods of economic crisis. This performance is attributed to its nature as a tangible good and its ability to serve as a store of value in times of uncertainty. Financial analysts often recommend maintaining a 5-10% allocation to gold in a diversified portfolio to protect against economic shocks (Elements by Visual Capitalist).

In conclusion, although gold is not completely immune to short-term price fluctuations, its history of performance during economic crises makes it a prudent choice for investors looking to protect their assets during times of instability. .

14.3 Advantages and disadvantages of investing in gold

Investing in gold has several advantages and disadvantages that investors should consider before deciding to include this precious metal in their portfolio. Here is a detailed analysis of the main points to consider.

Benefits of investing in gold

1. **Portfolio Diversification**
    - **Risk Reduction** : Gold provides effective diversification because it tends to have a low or negative correlation with stocks and bonds. In times of financial market volatility, gold can reduce overall portfolio risk.
    - **Protection against Inflation** : Gold has historically preserved its value during periods of inflation. When prices rise, gold tends to maintain its purchasing power, acting as a hedge against monetary erosion (US Money Reserve).

AI Bubble: How to Survive the Next Stock Market Crash

2. **Liquidity and Portability**
   - **Ease of Sale** : Gold is easily sold on world markets. Investors can quickly convert their assets into cash without significant loss of value.
   - **Transport Facile** : Unlike other tangible assets like real estate, gold is easily transportable, making it convenient for international investors or those seeking geographic flexibility.
3. **Safety in Times of Uncertainty**
   - **Stability in Times of Crisis** : In times of economic or geopolitical crisis, gold tends to maintain or even increase its value, providing security to investors.
   - **No Debt** : Physical gold is not affected by counterparty or default risks, unlike other financial instruments such as stocks or bonds (US Money Reserve).

Disadvantages of investing in gold

1. **Lack of Yield**
   - **No Income** : Gold does not generate passive income like dividends from stocks or interest from bonds. Investors can only benefit from a return through the appreciation of the price of gold.
   - **Conservation Costs** : Holding physical gold can incur storage and insurance costs, reducing potential gains.
2. **Price Volatility**
   - **Market Fluctuations** : Although gold is often seen as a safe haven, it can also be subject to significant price volatility, influenced by market speculation and monetary policies.
   - **Reactions to Interest Rates** : Changes in interest rates can affect gold prices. Higher interest rates make income-generating assets more attractive, which can reduce demand for gold and lower its price (US Money Reserve).
3. **Tax Complexity**

- **Taxation of Capital Gains** : In some countries, gains made from the sale of gold are subject to capital gains taxes, which can reduce net returns for investors.
- **Regulations** : Regulations surrounding the buying, selling and storage of gold can vary significantly from country to country, adding a layer of complexity for international investors.

Conclusion

Investing in gold offers significant benefits, particularly in terms of diversification, security in times of uncertainty and liquidity. However, it also has disadvantages such as lack of yield, price volatility and tax complexity. Investors should evaluate these factors based on their financial goals and risk tolerance before deciding to include gold in their portfolio.

14.4 Comparison with other safe havens

When it comes to protecting investments during times of economic uncertainty, several assets are often considered safe havens. Besides gold, these assets include silver, Treasury bonds, consumer staples stocks, and more recently, cryptocurrencies like Bitcoin. Each asset class has unique advantages and disadvantages. Here is a detailed comparison based on the key characteristics of these safe havens.

Or

- **Stability** : Gold has a long history of stability and is considered a reliable hedge against inflation and economic turmoil. Its value tends to increase when financial markets are in difficulty, making it a haven for investors looking for security.

- **Liquidity** : Gold is highly liquid, with deep and active markets. Investors can easily buy and sell gold in the form of bars, coins or ETFs.
- **Storage Costs** : Storing physical gold may incur additional costs for security and insurance. These costs must be taken into account when evaluating the investment in gold (The Royal Mint) (Trakx).

Money

- **Industrial Use** : Silver, like gold, is a safe haven, but it also benefits from significant industrial demand. This can provide additional stability during times of economic growth.
- **Affordable Price** : Silver is often more affordable than gold, making it easier for small investors to access. However, its volatility may be higher due to its dual industrial and investment use (Scottsdale Bullion & Coin).
- **Historical Performance** : Silver tends to follow the movements of gold, but with increased volatility. It can offer high returns, but also greater risks (Trakx).

Treasury Bonds

- **Security** : U.S. Treasury bonds are considered one of the safest investments, being backed by the United States government. They offer fixed returns and are less volatile than stocks or commodities.
- **Yield** : Although safe, Treasury bonds generally offer lower yields, especially in a low interest rate environment. They are ideal for investors looking to preserve capital with minimal risk.
- **Liquidity** : Treasury bonds are very liquid and can be easily bought and sold in secondary markets (Scottsdale Bullion & Coin).

Consumer Staples Stocks

- **Resilience** : Consumer staples stocks, like those of companies producing essential goods (food, personal care), tend to perform well even during recessions because demand for their products remains constant.
- **Dividends** : Many of these companies pay regular dividends, providing stable passive income to investors.
- **Lower Risks** : Although less volatile than growth stocks, consumer staples stocks are not completely immune to market shocks (Scottsdale Bullion & Coin).

Bitcoin

- **High Volatility** : Bitcoin is extremely volatile compared to gold and other traditional safe havens. This volatility can provide opportunities for high returns, but also presents significant risks.
- **Accessibility** : Bitcoin can be purchased in fractions, making it accessible to a wide range of investors. Transactions are fast and can be carried out 24/7.
- **Security and Storage** : Secure storage of Bitcoins requires rigorous measures to protect private keys. The risks of cyberattacks and loss of keys must be considered (Trakx).

Conclusion

Each safe haven has specific advantages and disadvantages. Gold and silver are traditional safe havens offering stability and protection against inflation, but they can incur storage costs. Treasury bonds are extremely safe but offer lower yields. Consumer staples stocks provide resilience and steady dividends, while Bitcoin offers high return potential with significant volatility. Investors should evaluate their financial goals, risk tolerance and time horizon to choose the mix of assets that best suits their needs.

14.5 Expert Analysis: Gold Returns and Recession Protection

Gold is known for its ability to provide protection against economic uncertainties, particularly during periods of recession. Many financial and economic experts have analyzed gold's performance under these conditions and provide perspectives on its role as a safe haven asset.

Colossal investments by countries in gold

Several countries have invested heavily in gold to strengthen their economic sovereignty and protect themselves against financial market fluctuations and geopolitical uncertainties. For example, China and Russia have significantly increased their gold reserves in recent years. Russia, in particular, has accumulated significant quantities of gold to diversify its assets and reduce its dependence on foreign currencies, in response to economic sanctions and geopolitical tensions. Likewise, China has stepped up its gold purchases to support economic stability and strengthen its position in the global financial system (Gold.org) (IN).

Historical performance of gold during a recession

Gold has historically performed well during recessions. During the 2008 financial crisis, for example, gold saw its price rise significantly while other assets lost value. This trend has been repeated during the COVID-19 pandemic, where gold has reached all-time highs due to economic uncertainty and financial market disruptions (Gold.org) (IN).

Factors influencing the value of gold during recessions

Several factors contribute to gold's resilience during recessions:

- **Inflation and currency devaluation** : Gold serves as a hedge against inflation and currency devaluation. When central banks cut interest rates to stimulate the economy, the opportunity cost of holding gold decreases, making the asset more attractive to investors.

- **Economic uncertainty** : In times of volatility and economic uncertainty, gold is seen as a safe haven. Investors are flocking to gold to protect their capital against losses in the stock markets.

Expert opinions

Financial experts often recommend maintaining a gold allocation in a diversified portfolio to protect against recessions. Maxwell Gold of State Street Global Advisors points out that gold has historically outperformed stocks and bonds during recessions. Additionally, Jim Iuorio of CME Group notes that gold attracts liquidity during periods of recession, which helps stabilize investment portfolios (Gold.org) (IN).

Practical recommendations

To maximize the benefits of gold as a safe haven against recessions, experts suggest:

- **Diversification** : Maintaining a 5-10% allocation to gold in a portfolio can provide significant protection against market losses.
- **Long term investment** : Investing in gold with a long-term perspective helps smooth out short-term fluctuations and benefit from its ability to retain value over long periods (Gold.org) (IN).

In conclusion, gold continues to prove its value as a safe-haven asset during recessions, providing protection against inflation and economic uncertainties. The massive investments by countries like China and Russia in their gold reserves highlight the importance of this asset in managing economic risks. Individual investors can also leverage these lessons to secure their portfolios during times of crisis.

14.6 Gold Investment Strategies: Physical, ETF, Mining Stocks

When you think about investing in gold, there are several ways to do it, each with its own particularities and advantages. Physical gold, gold-linked ETFs, and gold mining company stocks are the main methods, and each attracts different types of investors for various reasons.

Physical Gold

Purchasing physical gold, whether in the form of bars, coins or even jewelry, is a traditional and tangible method of holding gold. The idea of having a tangible asset in their hands brings a certain psychological security to investors. In France, for example, the 20 gold franc coin, known as the "Napoleon", is very popular. This coin has a rich history and has long been considered a safe haven in times of economic crisis. The price of this coin has experienced significant variations over the years. In 2011, it reached around 250 euros during the gold price surge, and more recently, in 2024, it is trading around 330-350 euros, reflecting overall trends in gold markets (goldandenergyadvisor.com).

Gold Linked ETFs

Then there are ETFs (Exchange Traded Funds) which allow you to invest in gold without having to physically own it. ETFs are very popular among investors who prefer simplicity and liquidity. These funds track the price of gold and provide direct exposure to its price without the hassle associated with physically owning the metal. For example, SPDR Gold Shares (GLD) is one of the largest and most traded ETFs, providing a convenient way to invest in gold (goldandenergyadvisor.com).

Mining Stocks

Finally, investing in the stocks of gold mining companies is another way to harness the value of gold. Mining stocks can offer high returns, especially when gold prices rise, as mining company profits can grow disproportionately to the price of gold itself. However, there is also more volatility and risk associated with these investments, as mining companies face operational challenges, production costs, and geopolitical risks. Companies like Barrick Gold and Newmont Mining are among the largest and most recognized in this sector (goldandenergyadvisor.com).

In conclusion, whether purchasing physical gold, investing in ETFs, or choosing mining stocks, each method has its own attractions and considerations. Gold remains a popular and reliable investment for those looking to diversify their portfolio and protect against economic turmoil. The 20 franc gold coin is an excellent example of the durability and perceived value of gold over time.

14.7 Gold Investor Testimonials

Investing in gold attracts varied opinions among investors, with some of them sharing their experiences and opinions on the benefits and challenges associated with this investment. Here are some concrete testimonials and quotes from experts in the field.

Investor Testimonials

1. **Danny Moses, Porter Collins, and Vincent Daniel, famous for "The Big Short"**
    - These investors explained on CNBC why they are bullish on gold for the long term. They cited growing debt levels in the United States and the potential devaluation of the dollar as primary reasons for their preference for gold. Collins said, "Government debt is growing too fast. Just think about that dollar in your wallet. How much will it be worth tomorrow?" Moses added that he has a large long position in Sprott Physical Gold Trust, which is up 16% this year (markets.businessinsider.com).

2. **Eric Sterner, investment director at Apollon Wealth**
   - Eric Sterner was bullish on gold in 2024, due to persistent inflation, geopolitical tensions and prospects of interest rate cuts by the Fed. He pointed out that gold had returned an average of 20.19% during the last seven US recessions, saying "gold continues to be a safe haven in times of uncertainty" (InvestmentNews).
3. **Joe Cavatoni, chief market strategist for the World Gold Council**
   - Cavatoni highlighted strong demand from central banks and retail investors, particularly in India and China, as key factors in gold price stability. He said heavy buying by central banks had established a solid floor for gold prices at around $1,850 an ounce, and this trend is expected to continue in 2024 (InvestmentNews).

Examples and Anecdotes

1. **Anecdote from an Anonymous Investor**
   - An individual investor shared his experience buying gold coins during the 2008 financial crisis. He explained that "owning physical coins gave me a sense of security as financial markets collapsed around me ". This testimony highlights the peace of mind that investing in physical gold can provide during periods of economic turbulence.
2. **Thoughts from an Institutional Investor**
   - A fund manager discussed how he diversified his portfolio with gold to protect against systemic risks. "Gold has proven its value not only as a hedge against inflation but also as insurance against financial crises," he said in an interview with Investing News Network (IN).

Conclusion

These testimonials and opinions clearly illustrate why gold remains an attractive investment option for many investors, whether individual or institutional. Gold's ability to preserve value during times of crisis, combined with continued demand from central banks and investors, continues to reinforce its status as a safe haven. In 2024, with continued economic and geopolitical uncertainties, gold remains an essential pillar in prudent investment strategies.

Chapter 15: Should we take refuge in real estate?

In an economic context marked by uncertainties and fluctuations in the financial markets, real estate is often considered a safe haven for investors. Historically, real estate has proven its resilience and its ability to generate stable and attractive returns over the long term. This chapter explores why real estate could be a solid alternative to more volatile investments, like stocks or gold, during times of crisis.

15.1 Analysis of the current real estate market

Analysis of the real estate market in 2024 reveals a complex situation, influenced by various economic, geopolitical and social factors. Here's a look at the key trends and dynamics shaping the real estate market today.

Evolution of real estate prices

Property prices have seen significant increases in many parts of the world in recent years. This trend is largely due to increased demand for residential and commercial real estate, fueled by historically low interest rates and a lack of new construction in certain areas.

- **UNITED STATES** : In the United States, the real estate market continued to grow despite the interest rate increases announced by the Federal Reserve. Home prices rose 10% on average in 2023, but some major cities saw even steeper increases.
- **Europe** : In Europe, the real estate market remains robust, with notable increases in cities like Paris, Berlin and Madrid. The European Central Bank's low interest rate policies have supported this growth, although some regions are starting to show signs of overheating.

Factors influencing the market

Several factors play a key role in the current dynamics of the real estate market:

- **Interest rate** : The monetary policy of central banks directly influences the real estate market. Low interest rates make mortgages more affordable, increasing demand for real estate. However, recent interest rate hikes intended to combat inflation could curb this trend.
- **Inflation** : Inflation is another critical factor. In times of high inflation, real estate is often seen as a hedge against currency devaluation, as real estate assets tend to appreciate in value in tandem with inflation.
- **Urbanization and demography** : Population growth and continued urbanization in major global cities are creating sustained demand for housing. Migration to urban centers for employment opportunities and a better life is fueling the demand for residential and commercial housing.

Impact of the COVID-19 pandemic

The COVID-19 pandemic has had a profound impact on the real estate market, changing buyer and renter preferences. Demand for larger living spaces, often located on the outskirts of major cities, has increased, while city centers have seen a relative decline in demand due to teleworking and changes in lifestyles.

Institutional and foreign investments

Institutional investment in real estate continues to grow, with pension funds, insurance companies and sovereign wealth funds increasing their exposure to the sector. Additionally, foreign investment in real estate remains robust, attracted by the stability and potentially high returns of the real estate market in major cities.

Conclusion

The current real estate market offers attractive opportunities for investors looking for stability and long-term returns. However, it is essential to remain attentive to macroeconomic changes, such as interest rate policies and inflation, which can significantly influence market dynamics. By carefully evaluating these factors, investors can make informed decisions about how to incorporate real estate into their overall investment strategy.

15.2 Risks and opportunities in real estate in 2024

In 2024, the real estate market presents both significant risks and opportunities for investors. Understanding these dynamics is crucial to effectively navigating this industry.

Risks

1. **High interest rates and availability of capital**
    - Rising interest rates since 2022 have made credit more expensive and less accessible, reducing transaction volumes and increasing financing costs for real estate investors. About 50% of respondents to a Deloitte survey indicated that the cost of capital and availability of capital are major concerns for 2024, compared to 38% and 40% the previous year (Deloitte United States).
    - This situation can exacerbate the financial distress of owners of real estate assets, particularly those whose debts are maturing and who struggle to refinance on favorable terms.
2. **Transformation of the office market**
    - Demand for office space remains uncertain due to the widespread adoption of hybrid working. Vacancy rates reached 23% in business centers and 22% in the suburbs in the first quarter of 2024, with a drop in average rents of almost 2% year-on-year (Moss Adams).

- Companies' strategies vary, with some reducing their office footprint while others are investing in Class A office space with premium amenities to attract employees.
3. **ESG regulations and climate change costs**
    - Environmental, social responsibility and governance (ESG) requirements are becoming increasingly stringent, imposing additional costs on property owners and managers. In 2024, nearly 60% of real estate companies report not having the data and processes necessary to comply with ESG standards (Deloitte United States).
    - Extreme weather events also increase insurance costs, which can limit landlords' ability to raise rents or find adequate coverage (Barings).

Opportunities

1. **Investments in quality assets**
    - Despite economic challenges, there are opportunities to acquire high-quality real estate that meets the current needs of investors and tenants. For example, office buildings with modern, eco-friendly amenities continue to attract interest from tenants and investors (PwC).
    - Well-located and well-maintained real estate assets can offer stable and attractive returns, particularly those that can benefit from long-term trends such as urbanization and demand for sustainable housing.
2. **Adaptation to new market realities**
    - Investors who adapt to new market realities, such as growing demand for industrial and logistics space due to e-commerce and the relocation of supply chains, can find lucrative opportunities (Moss Adams) (PwC).
    - The industrial sector saw increased demand during and after the pandemic, with historically low vacancy rates, although this demand declined slightly in early 2024 due to the increased supply of new space (Moss Adams).
3. **Acquisitions of distressed properties**
    - Increased financial distress among owners of real estate assets provides opportunities for well-capitalized investors to repurchase properties at discounted prices.

In 2024, investors begin to position themselves to acquire undervalued assets, anticipating more favorable opportunities as prices continue to adjust (Deloitte United States) (Barings).

Conclusion

The real estate market in 2024 is marked by significant challenges, notably due to high interest rates and increasing ESG requirements. However, opportunities exist for investors who can adapt and target high-quality assets or take advantage of distressed properties. By staying informed and being willing to adjust their strategies, investors can effectively navigate this complex landscape and take advantage of emerging real estate market trends.

15.3 Signs of a real estate bubble

In 2024, real estate markets in France and the United States show signs of significant fluctuations, but talk of a new bubble remains controversial. Here is an overview of the key indicators that could signal a potential real estate bubble, with a focus on the markets of Paris and major American cities.

France

Since 2022, the French real estate market has seen a significant drop in prices, particularly in Paris. Apartment prices in the capital fell by around 7% between February 2023 and February 2024, while house prices fell by 6.9% over the same period. This decline reflects a correction after several years of sustained increase, but it is important to note that this decline was more marked in peri-urban areas and certain provincial towns such as Caen and Grenoble (Investropa) (Global Property Guide) (Bluesky Finance).

1. **Rapid decline in property prices** : The observed price declines can be seen as a sign of correction rather than a burst bubble. Prices have fallen following a period of strong growth, but remain high compared to historical levels.
2. **Reduction of transactions** : The number of sales has also fallen, with a 20% decrease in 2023 compared to the previous year. This drop in transactions indicates some caution among buyers, exacerbated by tighter credit conditions and high interest rates (Bluesky Finance).
3. **Stricter lending standards** : Unlike the pre-crisis period of 2008, lending standards are currently more rigid, limiting access to real estate credit. Mortgage rates have reached around 4%, making the purchase of real estate less accessible for many households (Bluesky Finance).

UNITED STATES

In the United States, cities like Phoenix, Austin and San Diego have also seen significant fluctuations. Prices experienced a rapid increase, followed by some correction.

1. **Price increase and stabilization** : After significant increases post-pandemic, prices are starting to stabilize or decrease slightly in some regions. This may indicate that the market is reaching a new equilibrium rather than an impending bubble.
2. **Request for specific properties** : Demand remains strong for specific types of properties, particularly those with outdoor spaces, which has been accentuated by post-pandemic lifestyle changes. This targeted demand can keep prices high in certain market segments (Investropa) (Notaries of France).

Conclusion

In summary, although the real estate market in France and the United States is showing signs of correction after rapid price increases, talk of a new bubble may be premature. Current conditions, such as stricter lending standards and pricing adjustments, instead suggest a market rebalancing. Investors should remain vigilant and closely monitor economic developments and credit policies to assess future risks and opportunities.

15.4 Impact of high interest rates and regulations

The impact of high interest rates and regulations on the real estate market is considerable, influencing both the accessibility of real estate loans and the general dynamics of the market. In 2024, these factors play a crucial role in determining real estate market trends in France and the United States.

High interest rates

High interest rates have several notable effects on the real estate market:

1. **Cost of credit** : When interest rates rise, the cost of mortgages rises as well. This makes borrowing more expensive for potential buyers, reducing their ability to purchase. For example, in France, mortgage rates reached around 4% in 2024, leading to a significant decrease in loan applications (Bluesky Finance).
2. **Reduced accessibility** : Households that could previously afford to purchase a home now find their options limited. In the United States, this situation is similar, with higher interest rates reducing the accessibility of mortgage credit for many potential buyers (Investropa).
3. **Market slowdown** : As a result, the real estate market is experiencing a slowdown. Property sales have declined, as evidenced by the 20% drop in transactions in France in 2023 (Bluesky Finance). This trend is also observable in the United States, where housing sales have declined due to higher financing costs.
4. **Extension of sales deadlines** : Due to higher costs and reduced demand, properties are staying on the market longer. In France, the average time to sell a property has increased, reaching 85 days in Paris in 2023 (Bluesky Finance).

Regulations

Regulations also play a crucial role in the dynamics of the real estate market:

1. **Strict lending standards** : In response to past crises, financial regulations have become stricter. More rigid lending standards limit access to credit, thereby reducing demand. In France, banks now require higher down payments and more rigorous proof of repayment capacity, which further restricts potential borrowers (Bluesky Finance).
2. **Environmental and ESG regulations** : Sustainability and social responsibility (ESG) requirements add additional costs for property owners and developers. Construction projects must now meet stricter environmental standards, which can increase development costs and reduce profitability (Bluesky Finance).
3. **Impact of monetary policies** : The monetary policies of central banks, aimed at controlling inflation, directly influence interest rates. Decisions by the European Central Bank and the US Federal Reserve have a direct impact on the cost of mortgage loans, thereby affecting demand and activity in the real estate market (Investropa).

Conclusion

The impact of high interest rates and regulations on the real estate market in 2024 is significant. Higher interest rates increase the cost of credit and reduce affordability for potential buyers, thereby slowing the market. Regulations, while essential for financial stability and environmental sustainability, add layers of complexity and cost for real estate investors. In France and the United States, these factors combined create a market environment where prudence and strategy are crucial to effectively navigate and take advantage of opportunities as they arise.

15.5 Comparison with other asset classes

When it comes to comparing real estate to other asset classes, it is essential to consider several factors, including yield, volatility and the specific characteristics of each type of investment. In 2024, the returns and dynamics of different asset classes show significant divergences, providing investors with various opportunities and challenges.

Real estate yield

Real estate traditionally offers stable and attractive returns, especially when interest rates are low. In 2024, despite higher interest rates, the real estate market presents varied opportunities depending on the type of real estate.

- **Residential** : The residential market remains resilient, although yields vary depending on location and demand. For example, rental yields in cities like Paris and New York continue to be attractive, despite a recent decline in property prices. Investments in well-located and well-maintained properties can offer gross returns of around 3-5% annually (DWS Asset Management).
- **Commercial** : Office and commercial spaces are more volatile due to changing work patterns post-pandemic. Class A offices with modern amenities continue to attract tenants, but vacancy rates remain high in many major cities, affecting yields (AQR Capital Management).
- **Industrial** : Industrial properties, including warehouses and distribution centers, are benefiting from the growth of e-commerce and supply chains. This segment shows robust returns, often above 6%, due to sustained demand (DWS Asset Management).

Comparison with stocks

Stocks offer higher return potential, but with increased volatility. In 2023, stock returns have been mixed, with overall performance below expectations due to economic uncertainties. Technology and growth stocks have particularly suffered from rising interest rates, reducing valuations.

- **Expected return** : Mid-term equity return forecasts are around 5-7% annually, but with significant volatility depending on macroeconomic conditions and company performance (AQR Capital Management).
- **Dividends** : Dividend paying stocks can offer regular income, similar to rental income from real estate, but with a risk of stock price fluctuations.

Comparison with bonds

Bonds, especially government bonds, are considered safe investments with fixed returns. In 2024, bond yields have risen in response to central banks' rising interest rate policies, providing more competitive returns compared to previous years.

- **Expected return** : Government bonds offer yields of around 2 to 4%, depending on the maturity and the issuing country. Corporate bonds can offer higher yields, but with increased credit risk (AQR Capital Management).
- **Security** : Bonds are less volatile than stocks and real estate, providing relative stability to investment portfolios.

Comparison with alternative assets

Alternative assets, such as commodities, cryptocurrencies and hedge funds, offer opportunities for diversification and potentially high returns, but with high risks and increased complexity.

- **Raw materials** : Gold and other commodities can serve as a hedge against inflation and economic uncertainties, with variable returns depending on market conditions.

- **Cryptocurrencies** : Cryptocurrencies are extremely volatile and speculative, offering high potential returns but with significant risks of loss (AQR Capital Management).

Conclusion

In conclusion, each asset class has distinct advantages and disadvantages. Real estate offers stable, tangible returns, but can be affected by interest rates and economic cycles. Stocks offer high growth potential, but with increased volatility. Bonds provide relative security with fixed returns. Alternative assets offer diversification opportunities, but with added risks and complexity. Investors should evaluate their financial goals, risk tolerance and time horizon to determine the optimal mix of these assets in their portfolio.

15.6 Expert opinions on the future of real estate

Real estate market experts offer varied perspectives on the future of this sector in 2024, highlighting both the challenges and opportunities that lie ahead. Here are some of the key opinions and analyzes gathered from real estate professionals and economic analysts.

1. Evolution of interest rates and real estate prices

High interest rates have been a major obstacle for buyers in 2023, reaching near two-decade highs. However, experts predict a slight decline in mortgage rates in 2024, which could improve affordability for buyers. According to Fannie Mae, 30-year mortgage rates could stabilize around 6.7% by the end of the year (Money).

This rate cut could lead to an increase in demand and keep housing prices high. Price projections for 2024 vary, but Fannie Mae projects a 6.1% price increase for the year, while the Mortgage Bankers Association estimates a 4.5% increase (Business Insider) (Money).

2. Impact of inventory and demand

One of the biggest challenges in the U.S. real estate market is the lack of inventory. According to a recent Zillow analysis, there are about 4.5 million homes short of reaching a healthy inventory level. This housing shortage continues to put pressure on prices, even with high interest rates (Business Insider).

In France, although real estate prices have decreased in certain regions since 2022, notably in Paris, the market remains tense with high demand for quality and well-located housing (Investropa) (Bluesky Finance).

3. Forecast for home sales

Experts expect a slight recovery in home sales in 2024. Danielle Hale, chief economist at Realtor.com, anticipates a gradual improvement in housing affordability thanks to falling mortgage rates and a gradual increase in inventory (Money). However, this recovery will likely be modest and buyers will continue to face cost and affordability challenges.

4. Specific market segments

Certain segments of the real estate market offer particular opportunities. For example, industrial properties, supported by the growth of e-commerce, continue to show robust returns. Similarly, Class A offices and data centers are attracting investor interest due to demand for modern, well-appointed spaces (Business Insider).

Conclusion

The future of the real estate market in 2024 looks promising with signs of interest rates stabilizing and a slight recovery in demand. However, challenges related to limited housing inventory and affordability persist. Experts recommend carefully monitoring macroeconomic developments and the policies of the Federal Reserve and central banks to anticipate trends in the real estate market. In France as in the United States, investors must remain vigilant and flexible to navigate this complex and constantly evolving landscape.

15.7 Real estate investment strategies during volatile times

Investing in real estate during times of economic volatility requires a careful and well-thought-out approach. Here are some key strategies for taking advantage of opportunities while minimizing risks.

1. Diversification of investments

Diversifying your real estate investments is essential to spreading risks. Instead of concentrating all your assets in a single property type or region, consider diversifying into different property types (residential, commercial, industrial) and different geographic locations.

- Example: A diversified real estate portfolio could include apartments in Paris, warehouses on the outskirts of major French cities, and offices in emerging markets like Bordeaux or Lyon (Business Insider) (Money).

2. Invest in quality assets

Focus on acquiring high-quality real estate. Well-located, well-maintained and modern properties tend to better withstand market fluctuations and attract stable tenants.

- Example: Class A office buildings, residences in desirable neighborhoods, and modern industrial properties benefit from consistent demand even during volatile times (Business Insider) (Money).

3. SCPIs and Crowdfunding

In France, Real Estate Investment Companies (SCPI) and real estate crowdfunding offer interesting opportunities to diversify risks and optimize returns. Here is an overview of real estate investment strategies in periods of volatility, with a focus on SCPIs and real estate crowdfunding.

Civil Real Estate Investment Companies (SCPI)

SCPIs, the French equivalent of Real Estate Investment Trusts (REITs), allow investors to buy shares in companies that own and manage a diversified portfolio of rental real estate. They are popular in France for several reasons:

- **Diversification** : SCPIs invest in a wide range of real estate (offices, businesses, residences, warehouses), spread over different geographical regions, which reduces the risk associated with a single type of property or a single location.
- **Regular income** : SCPIs regularly distribute net rental income to their investors, providing a stable cash flow even in periods of volatility.
- **Professional management** : SCPIs are managed by specialized management companies, which take care of property selection, rental management and maintenance, allowing investors to benefit from their expertise without the constraints of direct management.

Rankings of the Best SCPIs and their Returns in 2024

Nom de la SCPI	Société de gestion	Taux de Distribution (TD) 2024	Type d'actifs
Transitions Europe	Arkea Reim	7.50%	Bureaux, commerces
Iroko Zen	Iroko	6.75% - 7.50%	Diversifié
Novaxia Neo	Novaxia Investissement	6.51%	Réhabilitation de bureaux
Épargne Pierre Europe	Atland Voisin	6.26%	Bureaux, commerces, logistique
Remake Live	Remake AM	7.25% - 7.75%	Diversifié
Activimmo	Alderan	6.02%	Logistique, industriel
Cœur de Régions	Sogenial Immobilier	6.20%	Diversifié, régions
Cœur d'Europe	Sogenial Immobilier	5.93%	Diversifié, zone Euro
Cœur de Ville	Sogenial Immobilier	5.30%	Commerces, bureaux

Real estate crowdfunding

Real estate crowdfunding allows individuals to finance real estate projects by contributing to crowdfunding platforms. This type of investment has several advantages and disadvantages:

- **Access to diversified projects** : Crowdfunding makes it possible to invest in a variety of real estate projects, ranging from residential construction to the renovation of commercial buildings, with relatively small investment amounts.
- **Potential for high returns** : Real estate crowdfunding projects can offer attractive returns, often higher than traditional real estate investments, due to the higher risks associated with the development phase.

- **Risk of capital loss** : The main disadvantage of real estate crowdfunding is the risk of capital loss, especially if the project fails or if the developer goes bankrupt. It is crucial to carefully evaluate projects and platforms before investing.

Examples of real estate crowdfunding platforms in France

1. **Homunity** : French real estate crowdfunding platform which offers a wide range of projects, ranging from residences to offices. Homunity stands out for its transparency and its rigorously selected projects.
2. **I am shaking** : Another popular platform that allows investors to participate in real estate development projects in France. Anaxago offers varied investment options and emphasizes the quality and viability of projects.

4. Focus on income-generating properties

Investing in properties that generate regular rental income can provide stability during periods of volatility. Well-located residential and commercial properties with strong leases can provide consistent cash flow.

- Example: Renting apartments in college towns or offices to strong businesses can provide a stable and predictable source of income (Business Insider).

5. Prudent financing strategies

In times of volatility, it is crucial to prudently manage the financing of your real estate investments. Avoid over-leveraging your properties and opt for fixed interest rates to protect against fluctuations in variable rates.

- Tip: Working with reputable lenders and securing favorable financing terms can help maintain financial stability even if market conditions deteriorate (Money).

6. Invest in renovations and improvements

Improving existing properties can increase their value and attractiveness to tenants. Targeted renovations, such as improving energy efficiency or upgrading facilities, can attract quality tenants and justify higher rents.

- Example: Installing efficient heating and cooling systems, updating kitchens and bathrooms, or improving insulation can make a property more attractive and increase its rental value (Business Insider).

7. Stay Informed and Adaptable

Real estate markets can change quickly, especially during volatile times. It is crucial to stay informed about market trends, regulatory changes and economic conditions. Being prepared to adjust your investment strategies in response to new information is essential to success.

- Tip: Following market reports, economic analyzes and expert forecasts can help make informed decisions and anticipate emerging trends (Business Insider).

Conclusion

In times of volatility, especially if a stock market bubble is in sight, SCPIs and real estate crowdfunding offer interesting alternatives for diversifying real estate investments and reducing risks. SCPIs allow you to benefit from regular income and professional management, while real estate crowdfunding offers the possibility of accessing diversified projects with potentially high returns. However, it is essential to fully understand the risks associated with each type of investment and to choose quality projects and platforms.

Chapter 16: Divergent opinions: Correction or New Bubble?

The financial market, particularly technology stocks, is going through a period of great uncertainty in 2024. Analysts are divided on the nature of the recent fluctuations: are they a simple market correction or the harbingers of a new bubble speculative are they present? While some experts believe that the market naturally readjusts values following excessive valuations, others fear that we are on the verge of another collapse similar to previous bubbles. This chapter explores these divergent perspectives, focusing first on analyzing the current correction in technology stocks.

16.1 Analysis of the current correction of technology stocks

Since the start of 2023, technology stocks have seen significant fluctuations. After years of rapid growth, driven by constant innovation and historically low interest rates, the technology sector now appears to be in a readjustment phase.

Factors Contributing to Correction

1. **Rise in Interest Rates** : The US Federal Reserve and other global central banks have increased interest rates to combat inflation. This policy has made financing more expensive, reducing liquidity and slowing investments in technology stocks, traditionally more volatile and dependent on cheap financing.
2. **Overvaluation of Assets** : Technology stocks have reached very high valuation levels, often disconnected from economic fundamentals. Valuation multiples (such as the price-to-earnings ratio) were particularly high for technology companies, justified by sometimes unrealistic expectations of future growth.
3. **Reduction of Profits** : Tech companies, including giants like Meta, Amazon and Google, reported less spectacular financial

results than expected. Development and innovation costs, combined with increased competition, have squeezed profit margins.
4. **Geopolitical and Regulatory Incidents** : Geopolitical tensions, particularly between the United States and China, and stricter regulations regarding data and monopolies, have also impacted the performance of technology stocks. Technology companies face increasingly complex regulatory environments, affecting their ability to operate freely and grow internationally.

Perspectives des Experts

- **Optimists** : Some analysts see this correction as a necessary and healthy adjustment to the market, making it possible to eliminate excesses and return to more reasonable valuations. They believe the fundamentals of the technology sector remain strong, with continued demand for technological innovations and digital services.
- **Pessimists** : Other experts fear this correction is just the start of a deeper decline, suggesting tech stocks were overvalued in ways similar to the dotcom bubble of the 2000s. They warn of increased volatility and potential prolonged devaluation.

Impact on Investors

For investors, this correction is both a source of concern and an opportunity. On the one hand, it reminds us of the risks associated with investments in high-growth and high-volatility sectors. On the other hand, it offers purchasing opportunities at potentially depreciated prices for those who believe in the resilience and long-term potential of technologies.

Conclusion

Analysis of the current correction of technology stocks shows a complex dynamic influenced by macroeconomic, geopolitical and sectoral factors. Whether it's a simple correction or warning signs of a new bubble, it's crucial for investors to stay informed and reevaluate their strategies based on market developments.

16.2 Arguments Against the Existence of an AI Speculative Bubble and a Near Crisis

Several analysts and experts argue that AI is not currently in an impending speculative bubble. Here are arguments and analyzes that go in this direction:

1. Market Viability and Deep Integration AI is deeply integrated into many sectors such as healthcare, finance, and supply chain management, where it concretely improves efficiency and outcomes. For example, AI-powered diagnostic tools improve patient care, and fraud detection algorithms strengthen financial security. This integration shows adoption based on real value and not pure speculation.

2. Technological Maturity and Innovation AI benefits from technological maturity and rapid innovation, which supports its long-term growth. Continuing advances in machine learning algorithms and neural networks are constantly increasing the functionality and applicability of AI. Additionally, related technologies like cloud computing and the Internet of Things (IoT) are driving this growth, demonstrating that AI is far from a passing fad.

3. Global Adoption and Scalability The global adoption of AI and its ability to adapt to different markets and regulatory environments illustrates its long-term viability. AI technologies are used not only in developed economies but also in emerging markets, demonstrating their flexibility and potential for universal impact.

4. Strong Financial Foundations of Market Leaders Leading AI companies, such as Nvidia, Microsoft, and Google, have strong financial foundations with strong cash flow and continued investments in research and development. This financial stability suggests that current valuations are supported by strong fundamentals rather than excessive speculation.

5. Ethical and Regulatory Landscape The ethical implications and regulatory responses to AI play a crucial role in the perception of its

stability. Effective regulations that promote transparency, fairness and accountability can strengthen public trust and the stability of AI investments, reducing the risk of bubble conditions.

References:

- DigitalDefynd: 10 Factors That Matter
- The Motley Fool: Is the AI Bubble Popping? Don't Be so Sure
- Techopedia: The Skeptics Who Believe AI Is a Bubble

These arguments suggest that AI is well positioned for sustainable growth, supported by practical use and continued technological advances, allaying fears of a looming speculative bubble.

16.3 Growth Prospects for Technology Companies

The growth outlook for technology companies in 2024 is marked by unique challenges and opportunities. Despite a period of readjustment and volatility, technology fundamentals remain strong, supported by continued demand for innovation and digital transformation. Artificial intelligence (AI), in particular, plays a central role in the sector's growth prospects, particularly for the technology giants often referred to as the "sublime seven": Amazon, Apple, Google (Alphabet), Microsoft, Meta, Nvidia , and Tesla.

Positive Factors for Growth

1. **Digital Transformation and Technology Adoption**
    - Digital transformation continues to accelerate across all sectors. Amazon and Microsoft, for example, are investing heavily in cloud computing and AI technologies

to improve operational efficiency and customer experience. Amazon Web Services (AWS) and Microsoft Azure are well positioned to benefit from this continuing trend.
2. **Expansion of 5G Networks**
    - 5G adoption opens new possibilities for emerging technologies like the Internet of Things (IoT), self-driving cars, and augmented/virtual reality (AR/VR). Tesla, with its autonomous vehicles, and Apple, with its potential AR/VR projects, are well positioned to benefit from the expansion of 5G.
3. **Artificial Intelligence and Machine Learning**
    - AI and machine learning continue to revolutionize industries, from healthcare to finance to retail. Nvidia, as a leader in graphics processing units (GPUs) used for AI and machine learning, and Google (Alphabet) with its advances in AI through Google AI and DeepMind, are well positioned to see continued growth due to increased adoption of AI in business processes and consumer products.
4. **E-commerce and Digitalization of Commerce**
    - E-commerce remains a major driving force, with growing adoption by consumers across the world. Amazon and Alibaba continue to dominate this sector, while digital payment solutions and fintechs, such as those offered by Apple Pay, are also seeing sustained growth.

Challenges and Obstacles to Overcome

1. **Government Regulations and Controls**
    - Technology companies face increased regulation regarding data protection, privacy, and antitrust practices. Regulators in the United States, Europe, and Asia are imposing tighter constraints on large technology companies like Meta (formerly Facebook), limiting their ability to grow unhindered.
2. **Concurrence Intense**

- The technology sector is highly competitive, with relatively low barriers to entry in certain sub-segments. Businesses must continually innovate to maintain their competitive advantage, which can be costly and risky. Google and Microsoft, for example, compete directly in cloud services and AI technologies.
3. **Global Economic Fluctuations**
    - Macroeconomic uncertainties, such as inflation and supply chain disruptions, can affect the growth prospects of technology companies. Increases in interest rates, for example, make capital more expensive, which can dampen investment in R&D and expansion.

Investment Opportunities

1. **Innovative Startups and Niche Technologies**
    - Investors are looking for promising startups and niche technologies with high growth potential. Areas such as biotechnology, renewable energy, and digital health technologies offer attractive investment opportunities.
2. **Geographic Expansion**
    - Expanding into emerging markets, where technology penetration is still low but growing rapidly, presents a significant opportunity for technology companies. Markets in Asia, Africa, and Latin America offer immense growth potential.
3. **Merger and Acquisition**
    - Large technology companies continue to seek strategic acquisitions to strengthen their technological capabilities and market reach. Mergers and acquisitions in the technology sector can create synergies and open new avenues for growth. Nvidia, for example, recently acquired Arm Holdings to bolster its AI and processor capabilities.

Conclusion

Despite current challenges, the growth outlook for technology companies remains positive, supported by continued innovation and digital transformation. Companies that can navigate complex regulations, overcome intense competition, and take advantage of new technologies and emerging markets are well-positioned to thrive. Investors should remain attentive to industry trends and emerging opportunities to capitalize on the long-term growth potential of technologies.

16.4 Arguments from Wedbush analysts on the durability of the correction

Analysts at Wedbush, a leading financial analysis firm, recently released a series of reports on the current correction in technology stocks and its long-term impact. Their analysis focuses on several key aspects that could influence the sustainability of this correction.

1. Overvaluation of Technological Assets

Wedbush analysts point out that technology stocks were significantly overvalued before the correction. High valuations, often based on unrealistic future growth expectations, have led to extremely high valuation multiples (such as the price-to-earnings ratio).

- **Citation** : "The current correction is a necessary reaction to market excesses. Valuations must realign with stronger economic fundamentals," explains Daniel Ives, analyst at Wedbush.

2. Impact of Interest Rates

The Federal Reserve's increase in interest rates has had a significant effect on technology stocks. Wedbush analysts note that rising financing costs have reduced liquidity in markets and dampened investments in technology, traditionally more sensitive to changes in interest rates.

- **Citation** : "Technology stocks are particularly vulnerable to increases in interest rates. Companies must adjust their growth expectations and financing models accordingly," adds Ives.

3. Increased Competition and Regulatory Pressures

Intense competition in the technology sector, combined with increasing regulatory pressures, is another key factor in the correction. Regulators in the United States, Europe and Asia are placing tighter constraints on big tech companies, limiting their ability to grow unhindered.

- **Citation** : "Stricter regulations and increased oversight are hampering the expansion of large technology companies, adding an additional layer of risk for investors," says the Wedbush team.

4. Moderate Growth Outlook

Wedbush remains optimistic about the technology sector's long-term growth prospects, but with muted expectations. Analysts believe future growth will be more aligned with economic fundamentals, with continued adoption of artificial intelligence, 5G, and the Internet of Things (IoT) as key drivers.

- **Citation** : "We expect sustained growth in innovative segments like AI and 5G, but investors should be prepared for more realistic growth rates," concludes Daniel Ives.

5. Business Resilience Strategies

Wedbush analysts recommend that technology companies focus on resilience and innovation to navigate through this correction period. Companies that successfully adapt their strategies to new economic and regulatory realities will be better positioned to benefit from the recovery.

- **Citation** : "Technology companies must invest in innovation while building operational resilience to overcome current and future challenges," advises the Wedbush team.

Conclusion

Wedbush analysts consider the current correction in technology stocks to be sustainable and necessary to realign valuations with economic fundamentals. Although high interest rates and regulatory pressures present challenges, the growth outlook remains positive for innovative segments of the industry. Companies that focus on resilience and innovation will be best positioned to navigate through this correction period and emerge stronger.

16.5 Growth Predictions for Tech Stocks

In 2024, despite economic uncertainties and the recent market correction, many analysts forecast sustained growth of 15 to 20% for technology stocks. This prediction is based on several key factors that continue to propel the technology sector to new heights. Here's a look at the main reasons why tech stocks are likely to see robust growth in the years to come.

1. Accelerating the Adoption of Artificial Intelligence

Artificial intelligence (AI) is one of the most powerful drivers of technological growth. Technology companies are investing heavily in AI to improve their products and services, thereby increasing their efficiency and competitiveness.

- **Examples** :
    - **Nvidia** : A leader in graphics processing units (GPUs) and AI solutions, Nvidia continues to innovate with products like its A100 and H100 chips, widely used in data centers and AI applications.
    - **Alphabet (Google)** : With its subsidiaries Google AI and DeepMind, Alphabet conducts advanced research in AI, integrating these technologies into products such as Google Assistant and online advertising solutions.

2. Expansion du Cloud Computing

Cloud computing remains a growing sector, offering significant growth opportunities for technology companies. Cloud services enable businesses of all sizes to deploy solutions in a flexible and scalable manner.

- **Examples** :
    - **Amazon Web Services (AWS)** : As the cloud market leader, AWS continues to grow with new services and an expanding customer base.
    - **Microsoft Azure** : Microsoft Azure competes with AWS, offering robust cloud solutions for businesses and governments around the world.

3. 5G deployment

5G opens the door to new technological applications, including the Internet of Things (IoT), self-driving cars, and augmented/virtual reality (AR/VR). This new generation of mobile connectivity is driving demand for advanced technologies.

- **Examples** :
    - **Apple** : With its 5G-enabled iPhones, Apple is well positioned to take advantage of the rapid adoption of this technology.
    - **Tesla** : 5G facilitates the development and deployment of Tesla's autonomous vehicles, improving the connectivity and capabilities of smart cars.

4. Growth of E-Commerce and Fintechs

E-commerce and financial technologies (fintech) continue to transform consumer habits and financial services. The digitalization of commerce and financial services offers enormous growth potential for technology companies.

- **Examples** :

- **Amazon** : The undisputed leader in e-commerce, Amazon continues to expand its services, including Amazon Prime and Amazon Fresh.
- **PayPal** : Innovator in digital payments, PayPal is benefiting from the growth of online transactions and contactless payment solutions.

5. Innovations in Augmented/Virtual Reality and IoT

Augmented reality (AR), virtual reality (VR), and Internet of Things (IoT) technologies are opening new frontiers for technology companies. These innovations are creating opportunities in various sectors, including education, entertainment, and healthcare.

- **Examples** :
  - **Microsoft** : With HoloLens, Microsoft is exploring applications of mixed reality in industry and education.
  - **Alphabet (Google)** : Google's investments in AR/VR technologies, such as Google Glass, show the potential of these innovations.

Growth Analytics Projections

1. **Amazon**
   - **Growth prediction** : 15-17 %
   - **Factors** : Continued expansion of AWS, innovation in logistics and delivery, diversification of products and services.
2. **Apple**
   - **Growth prediction** : 15-18 %
   - **Factors** : Strong demand for flagship products (iPhone, iPad, Mac), growth in services (App Store, Apple Music), and innovations in AR/VR.
3. **Google (Alphabet)**
   - **Growth prediction** : 16-19 %

    - **Factors** : Leadership in digital advertising, expansion of cloud services via Google Cloud, and innovations in AI.
4. **Microsoft**
    - **Growth prediction** : 17-20 %

Conclusion

Predictions of 15-20% growth for tech stocks in 2024 are supported by continued innovations and increasing adoption of emerging technologies. Technology companies, including the "sublime seven" – Amazon, Apple, Google (Alphabet), Microsoft, Meta, Nvidia, and Tesla – are well positioned to take advantage of these trends. Investors should closely monitor developments in these areas to capitalize on the technology sector's long-term growth potential.

16.6 An Extended View of Stock Market Capitalization Forecasts: The Technological Titans at the Dawn of a New Era

The technology industry, already a central pillar of the global economy, appears poised to cross new historic thresholds in the years to come. Current forecasts, based on in-depth analyzes[8], indicate that several technology giants could reach unprecedented market capitalizations between 2024 and 2025, strengthening their position as undisputed leaders.

---

[8]https://www.tradingsat.com/nvidia-US67066G1040/actualites/nvidia-et-si-nvidia-devenait-la-premiere-entreprise-a-franchir-les-4000-milliards-de-dollars-de-capitalisation-1121264.html

NVIDIA: Towards 4000 Billion Dollars

NVIDIA is leading the discussion with a bold prediction: the possibility of becoming the first company in the world to reach a market capitalization of **4 trillion dollars**.

Currently valued around **1200 billion dollars** (August 2024), the company has seen its growth fueled by the rise of artificial intelligence, an area in which it plays a crucial role thanks to its graphics processing units (GPU). These GPUs are not only essential for gaming, but especially for training AI models, which require immense computing power.

The data center market, which is expected to reach a value of **$948 billion by 2030**, is another key driver for NVIDIA. With increasing infrastructure needs to support data processing and artificial intelligence capabilities, demand for NVIDIA products could continue to grow exponentially.

Apple, Microsoft and Alphabet: Firmly Anchored Titans

Apple, the first company to have crossed the threshold of **3 trillion dollars** capitalization, continues to show impressive solidity. With a current capitalization of **2850 billion dollars**, Apple is driven by the constant innovation of its products, exceptional loyalty from its customers, and the continued expansion of its ecosystem of services. Forecasts indicate the company could meet or even exceed **3500 billion dollars** in the coming years, thanks to initiatives such as augmented reality glasses and the continued development of its cloud services.

Microsoft, for its part, maintains a capitalization around **2500 billion dollars**, reinforced by dominance in cloud computing with Azure, and expansion in artificial intelligence with OpenAI. Rapid growth in its cloud and AI segments could see Microsoft reach **3 trillion dollars** by 2025, positioning the company as a key player in the digital economy.

Alphabet, Google's parent company, currently stands at around **1850 billion dollars**. Although a little behind its peers, the company benefits from the diversification of its revenues, notably in the cloud (Google Cloud), digital advertising, and increasingly, AI. Strong demand for cloud services, combined with improving profit margins in its advertising businesses, could propel Alphabet towards a capitalization of **2500 billion dollars** by 2025.

Economic Consequences and Opportunities

The rise of these giants is not just about the numbers, but also about the overall economic impact. The continued success of these companies could create positive ripple effects on national economies, boosting innovation, productivity and jobs in technology sectors.

However, this rapid growth is not without risks. High valuations can raise concerns about possible overvaluation, particularly in a high interest rate environment. Nevertheless, the diversification of these companies' revenue sources, their technological leadership, and their ability to innovate seem to prepare a bright future for the technology sector as a whole.

In conclusion, the forecast for 2024-2025 shows a technology sector that is not only resilient, but also expanding, with leaders like NVIDIA, Apple, Microsoft, and Alphabet poised to redefine the heights of market capitalization. Investors who bet on these giants could well see exceptional returns as the digital economy continues to grow and transform.

16.7 Strategies for Taking Advantage of Correction

The Subtle Art of Leveraging Disruptions

In the vast theater of the global economy, cycles of prosperity and recession follow one another with relentless regularity, like a tide that advances and recedes. Market corrections, although feared by some, are welcomed by others as invaluable opportunities. They act like the natural forces of an ecosystem, regulating excesses and restoring balance. In this cosmic order of things, the most sagacious investors do not fear storms, but see in them the opportunity to strengthen their positions, to buy back what others abandon in panic, and to sow the seeds of future wealth in the fertile soils of declining markets.

History has shown that the greatest financial successes often emerge from turbulent times. Savvy investors, such as Warren Buffett, whose shadow looms over every correction, know that it is precisely in moments of uncertainty that the contours of great fortunes take shape. The economy, as a living entity, feeds on these phases of readjustment to better redeploy itself. The strategies you are about to discover are not simple recipes for surviving a correction; they are the tools forged by experience and wisdom, intended to transform adversity into advantage, to make the storm an ally.

It is with this state of mind that I offer you this little summary (at the risk of repeating myself) of the **strategies to take advantage of the correction**. These strategies, imbued with realism and pragmatism, are designed to guide you through the stormy waters of crisis markets, providing you not only with the protection you need, but also with the means to thrive in a changing world:

1. **Invest in Quality Stocks** : Look for companies with strong fundamentals, prudent management, and a history of profitability. These stocks tend to recover more quickly after a correction.
2. **Diversify your Portfolio** : Don't put all your eggs in one basket. Diversify across different sectors, geographies, and asset classes (stocks, bonds, real estate, etc.) to reduce overall risk.
3. **Buy Stocks at Low Prices** : A market correction offers opportunities to buy quality stocks at a discount. Savvy investors, like Warren Buffett, often take advantage of these periods to acquire shares in undervalued companies.
4. **Adopt a Long-Term Vision** : Keep in mind that corrections are part of the economic cycle. Investors who take a long-term view, without panicking, are often those who obtain the best returns over time.

5. **Reassess the Risks** : Use the correction as an opportunity to reassess the risks in your portfolio. Adjust your positions to align with your risk tolerance.
6. **Monitor Liquidity Flows** : During corrections, monitor liquidity movements to spot sectors or companies that could benefit from a return of investors when conditions stabilize.
7. **Investing in Gold and Precious Metals** : Gold is often considered a safe haven in times of uncertainty. Investing in gold or other precious metals can provide protection against market volatility.
8. **Keep Cash in Reserve** : Having a cash reserve allows you to take advantage of buying opportunities when markets are down.
9. **Investing in Bonds** : Bonds can provide relative stability and a steady stream of income, especially when stock markets are volatile.
10. **Use Hedging Strategies** : Protect your portfolio from potential losses by using options or other derivative instruments.
11. **Monitor Institutional Investor Decisions** : Observe the movements of large investment funds, which often have sophisticated information and analysis at their disposal.
12. **Investing in Resilient Sectors** : Certain sectors, such as healthcare or consumer staples, are less affected by economic cycles and can offer protection against volatility.
13. **Profit from Market Anomalies** : Identify market anomalies or situations where stocks are oversold and have rebound potential.
14. **Stay Informed** : Knowledge is an asset. Follow economic and financial news to adapt your strategies according to market developments.
15. **Consider Index Funds or ETFs** : Investing in index funds or ETFs can provide diversified exposure to markets at a lower cost, while reducing the specific risk of a single stock.
16. **Review Your Retirement Plan** : Use corrections to adjust your retirement strategy, taking into account new economic realities and your investment horizon.

Adopt a Counter-Cyclical Approach:

As Warren Buffett has shown, being countercyclical—buying when others are selling and selling when others are buying—can provide opportunities to maximize long-term returns.

Each strategy requires careful thought and planning, as corrections can create both risks and opportunities. By taking a disciplined approach and sticking to a long-term vision, you can not only survive a correction, but also leverage it to strengthen your financial position.

16.8 Economic Analysis and Lessons from the Film The Big Short

The Big Short offers much more than a gripping tale of the 2008 financial crisis; it constitutes an in-depth study of the economic mechanisms which lead to the bursting of financial bubbles and stock market crashes. Through its characters, its events, and its analysis of the dysfunctions of the financial system, the film offers several crucial lessons for investors and regulators, particularly in the face of contemporary speculative dynamics such as the artificial intelligence bubble.

Understanding the Warning Signs of a Bubble

One of the film's first lessons is the importance of recognizing the warning signs of a bubble. In the case of the subprime crisis, the protagonists identify major imbalances: high-risk mortgages, overvaluation of real estate assets, and excessive reliance on complex derivatives like CDOs. These elements are a reflection of excessive speculation which ultimately implodes the market.

In the current context, parallels can be drawn with the high valuations of technology companies, particularly those related to artificial intelligence. When an innovation attracts massive amounts of capital, it is crucial to analyze whether valuations are supported by strong fundamentals or whether they are based on inflated expectations.

AI Bubble: How to Survive the Next Stock Market Crash

The Need for Vigilance and Skepticism

The Big Short highlights the importance of remaining vigilant and skeptical, even during times of economic growth. The main characters, who bet against the market, demonstrate a unique ability to challenge prevailing opinions and analyze data in ways that others overlook. Their skepticism allows them to see what the majority does not want to admit: the underlying fragility of the real estate market.

This lesson is particularly relevant today, as financial markets continue to grow after years of accommodative monetary policies. Investors must constantly reassess risks and ask themselves whether asset increases are justified or whether they hide deep vulnerability.

Risk Management and the Importance of Diversification

The film also demonstrates that those who knew how to manage risk managed to get through the crisis successfully. Michael Burry, for example, puts hedges in place on his real estate investments, despite widespread disbelief. This approach to risk management is crucial to protect against the inevitable bursting of a bubble.

For contemporary investors, diversification and hedging risks across different financial instruments are essential strategies for navigating volatile markets. Market corrections provide opportunities, but only for those who have planned downside protection strategies.

The Consequences of Systemic Dysfunctions

The Big Short also highlights the dangers of systemic dysfunctions and financial excesses. The lack of adequate regulation, the complexity of financial products, and the complacency of rating agencies contributed to the 2008 crisis. This illustrates the need for effective regulation and increased transparency to prevent excesses and protect the 'economy.

Today, as new forms of speculation emerge around cutting-edge technologies, regulators must be vigilant to avoid repeating the mistakes of the past. A healthy financial system relies on regulation that prevents the formation of excessive bubbles while allowing innovation.

Riding the Waves of Crisis: Lessons for Investors

Finally, *The Big Short* teaches that, despite the severity of crises, it is possible to take advantage of them. Investors who anticipated the subprime collapse made substantial gains, proving that rigorous analysis and counter-cyclical stance-taking can be successful. In the current context, figures like Warren Buffett, known for his cautious approach and counter-cyclical investing, show that even in times of high volatility, it is possible to "ride the wave" by remaining faithful to a strategy of disciplined investment.

In conclusion, *The Big Short* is not only a historical account of the 2008 crisis; it's a survival manual for investors in a world where bubbles and crashes are inevitable realities. The film reminds us that the key to navigating these turbulent waters lies in vigilance, rigorous risk management, and a deep understanding of the underlying economic dynamics.

Chapter 17: Current Economic Weaknesses that would make the Stock Market Crash more serious than before.

17.1 Detailed Analysis of Current Economic Weaknesses and Risks of Stock Market Crash

The global economic situation in 2024 presents many weaknesses that could precipitate a major stock market crash, amplified by unprecedented levels of public and private debt and an erosion of household savings reserves.[9].

Global Economic Slowdown

The economic slowdown is palpable through several indicators. Signs of recession are increasing, notably with a rise in the unemployment rate and a contraction in industrial activity in several major economies. In the United States, for example, the unemployment rate rose to 4.5% in 2024, and industrial production fell 2% from the previous year. This deterioration of the real economy has direct repercussions on consumption and investments, creating a vicious circle which further aggravates the current recession.

Volatility of Financial Markets

---

[9] For more details and in-depth analysis, sources used include reports from **World Bank** a you **Business Insider**.

AI Bubble: How to Survive the Next Stock Market Crash

Volatility in financial markets is exacerbated by divergences in monetary policies between the major central banks. The US Federal Reserve (Fed) continues its policy of raising rates to combat inflation, while the Bank of Japan maintains low rates to stimulate its economy. This divergence creates uncertainty in global markets, encouraging speculative movements and increasing the risk of imprudent investments. As a result, volatility indices, such as the VIX, have reached levels similar to those seen during previous financial crises.

Extreme Positioning and Speculative Bubbles

The craze for artificial intelligence (AI) has led to an overvaluation of technology companies, creating a potential speculative bubble. High valuations, particularly in the semiconductor sector, are supported by growth expectations that could prove unrealistic if demand were to slow. At the same time, carry trades[10] Massive moves on the yen, fueled by low rates in Japan, risk causing panic selling if investors suddenly withdraw from these positions, thus amplifying stock market falls.

Cascade consequences:

- **High Interest Rates** : The restrictive monetary policy adopted by the Fed increases the cost of borrowing for businesses. This

---

[10] The **carry trade** is a financial strategy where an investor borrows in a currency with a low interest rate (such as the Japanese yen) to invest in another currency with a higher rate (such as the US dollar). The investor benefits from the rate difference between the loan and the investment. For example, if the rates are 0.1% in Japan and 5% in the United States, the investor can make a profit of almost 4.9% by investing in American bonds. However, this strategy carries risks, including fluctuating exchange rates and interest rates.

Risks include volatility in exchange rates, which may reduce or wipe out gains, and unexpected changes in interest rates, which may make the investment less profitable or even cause losses.

reduces their profitability and can lead to waves of layoffs, increasing pressure on the labor market and consumption.
- **Liquidity Shock** : The combination of massive asset sales and buyer reluctance in times of volatility could trigger a liquidity shock. Such a shock would cause asset prices to fall rapidly, compounding losses for financial institutions and investors.

Increased Economic Fragility: Debt and Savings

The fragility of the global economy is accentuated by record levels of public and private debt. In the United States, the public debt reached approximately **$33.2 trillion** in 2024, representing almost 98% of GDP, a level not seen since the Second World War. This massive debt limits governments' room for maneuver in the event of an economic crisis, thus increasing the risk of a crisis of confidence in the sovereign debt markets.

In addition, household savings reserves are falling significantly. In the United States, the household savings rate fell to **4,4 %** of their disposable income in April 2022, the lowest level since the Great Recession of 2008. This reduction in savings reserves makes consumers more vulnerable to economic shocks and reduces their ability to support demand during economic downturns.

Conclusion

Today's economic vulnerabilities are numerous and interconnected, creating an environment particularly ripe for a stock market crash. High country debt, low household savings reserves, and increased market volatility are all factors that could precipitate a major financial crisis if a triggering event were to occur. Economic decision-makers must therefore be extremely vigilant in the face of these systemic risks.

17.2 The Situation in France: Ability to Survive a Stock Market Crash

France, like many other major economies, faces a series of economic challenges that could make the country particularly vulnerable in the event of a stock market crash. By examining public debt, the household savings rate, and the resilience of the labor market, it is possible to get an idea of France's capacity to withstand such a crisis.

Public Debt and Budget Deficit

France's public debt has reached historically high levels, representing approximately **112% you PIB** in 2024. This massive debt, much of it accumulated during the COVID-19 pandemic, limits the government's ability to respond effectively in a crisis. The budget deficit, which exceeds **5% you PIB**, further reinforces this vulnerability. Such a situation would make it difficult to apply expansionary fiscal policies to support the economy during a stock market crash, increasing the risk of a prolonged recession.

Savings Rate and Household Consumption

The household savings rate in France is relatively stable but remains lower than the levels observed in other European countries such as Germany[11]. In 2023, this rate was approximately **16 %**[12], a slight decrease compared to previous years. This savings reserve could provide some buffer in the event of an economic crisis, but it would probably not be enough to offset a prolonged fall in consumption if unemployment were to rise significantly.

---

[11] France is still one of the countries in the euro zone with the highest savings rate (Germany: 20.4%; Spain: 13.1%; Italy: 8.9%) at the end of 2023.

[12] https://www.fbf.fr/fr/lepargne-des-menages-faits-et-chiffres-cles/

Labor Market and Economic Resilience

The labor market in France is showing signs of resilience, with a stable unemployment rate around **7,4 %** in 2024. However, an increase in layoffs, particularly in industrial and technology sectors, could quickly erode this stability. France has put in place mechanisms such as partial unemployment to cushion economic shocks, but these measures are costly and could be difficult to maintain if the crisis persists.

Resilience Capacity in the Face of a Crash

France's ability to survive a stock market crash will largely depend on how quickly and effectively the government and financial institutions respond. The Bank of France, in coordination with the ECB, could intervene to stabilize financial markets, but room for maneuver is limited by high public debt and budgetary constraints. In addition, the reaction of households and businesses will be crucial. If consumer and investor confidence deteriorates, the country could face a deep recession.

In summary, although France has certain tools to mitigate the impact of a stock market crash, its economy remains fragile. High public debt, dependence on robust domestic consumption, and the stability of the labor market will be determining factors in its ability to weather such a crisis. Increased vigilance and prudent management will be essential to minimize the effects of a possible market fall.

Some references on the subject:

Here is a list of recent sources and references that have been used to analyze the economic situation in France and the risks associated with a stock market crash:

1. **World Bank** - Analysis of global financial fragility, particularly the impact of public and private debt on emerging and developed economies:
    - Source : World Bank - Debt and Financial Fragility (World Bank)

2. **Business Insider** - An in-depth study on the impact of US public debt and how it could trigger a new financial crisis. This source made it possible to put into perspective the risks associated with high debt levels in developed economies like that of France:
    - Source : How Mounting US Debt Could Trigger the Next Financial Crisis - Business Insider (Business Insider)
3. **World Economic Forum** - A recent analysis of savings rates in the United States, which was compared to the French situation to understand the fragility of households in the face of an economic crisis:
    - Source : Inflation is Hitting Americans' Savings Hard - World Economic Forum (WEF Website)
4. **INSEE (National Institute of Statistics and Economic Studies)** - For data specific to France, including the unemployment rate, household savings rate, and other key economic indicators:
    - Source: INSEE - Key figures of the French economy

17.3 Inevitability of Corrections: The Threat of Cycles

Even if the global economy manages to avoid the sudden bursting of the artificial intelligence bubble, it is almost certain that market corrections will occur, probably as early as 2025. These corrections, which could be more or less severe, are anchored in the cyclical dynamics of the economy, in particular the Juglar and Kondratieff cycles.

AI Bubble: How to Survive the Next Stock Market Crash

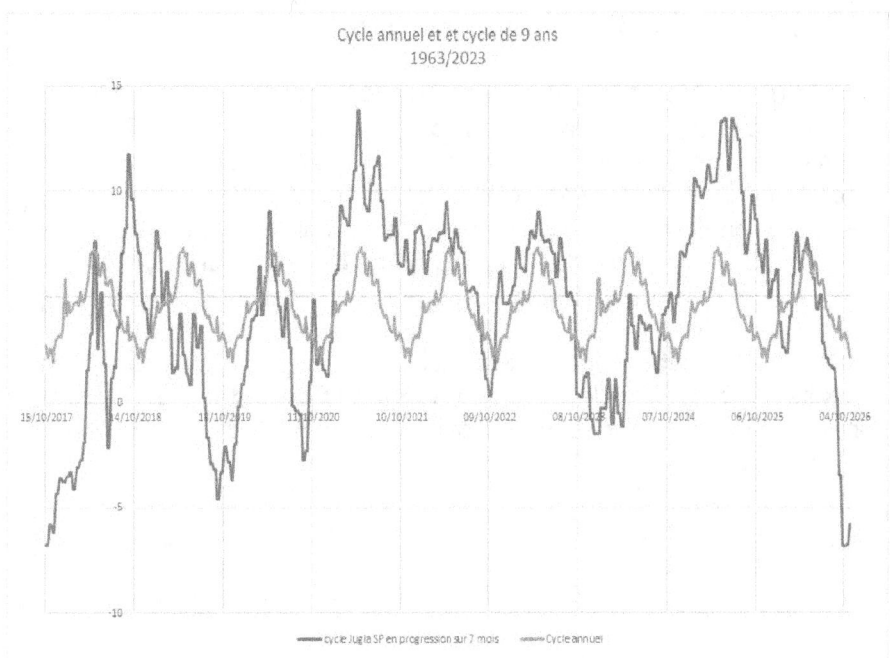

Source : Christian Guy
http://bourse-previsions-nyse-obama-2012.over-blog.com/2023/09/cycle-juglar-de-9-ans-et-bourses.html

The Correction at the end of 2025: An Inevitable Readjustment

With valuations in the technology sector skyrocketing, driven by the AI craze, the market could see a significant correction in 2025. This correction would be the result not only of the end of a Juglar cycle but also of the confluence of economic pressures and realistic expectations regarding future returns. Additionally, as the Kondratieff cycle of technological innovation matures, opportunities for rapid growth may diminish, leading to more frequent and intense market adjustments.

These corrections will not necessarily be catastrophic, but they will be essential to realign investor expectations with economic reality. Business cycles, such as those described by Juglar and Kondratieff, serve as reminders that phases of growth and contraction are natural and, although difficult, necessary to maintain long-term economic balance.

Conclusion: Preparing for the Inevitable

In conclusion, even without a sudden burst of the AI bubble, the market will not be able to escape significant corrections in the future. The business cycles of Juglar and Kondratieff, well documented in economic theory, indicate that 2025 could be a pivotal year where a major correction could occur. Investors and economic policymakers must be aware of these cyclical dynamics and prepare accordingly, by diversifying their investments and adopting appropriate risk management strategies.

To learn more about business cycles and their impact on financial markets, sources include works on **economic cycle theories** and recent reports from economic analysts available on platforms such as **World Economic Forum** And **S&P Global**.

17.4 The 6th Wave of Innovation: A New Technological Era in Perspective

While the Juglar and Kondratieff cycles offer an overview of economic dynamics in the medium and long term, the theory of waves of innovation, in particular the 6th wave of innovation, provides a more specific perspective on technological transformations and current economic conditions.

What is the 6th Wave of Innovation?

The innovation wave theory, popularized by economist Joseph Schumpeter, suggests that technological innovation occurs in cycles, each having a major impact on the global economy. The 6th wave, which is currently emerging, is characterized by a convergence of advanced technologies and increased awareness of environmental and societal challenges.

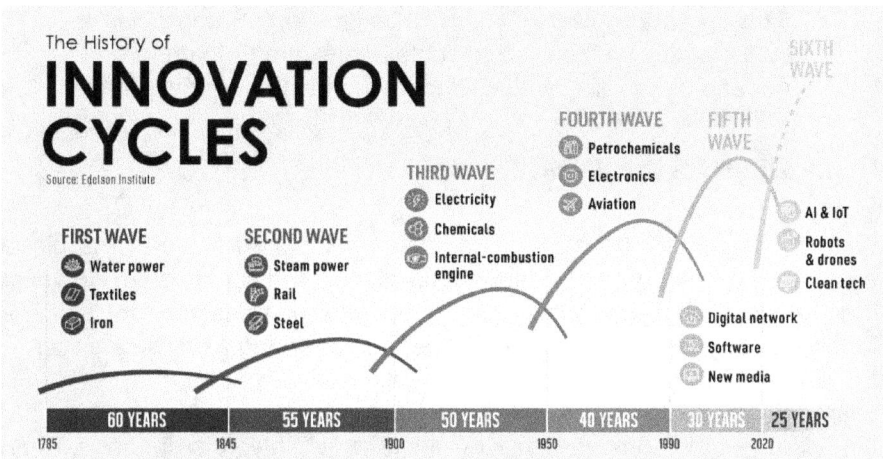

Source : Visual Capitalist

According to the article from *Visual Capitalist*, this new wave is powered by technologies such as artificial intelligence (AI), the Internet of Things (IoT), renewable energy, and biotechnology. Unlike previous waves, which were mainly focused on industry, the 6th wave is distinguished by a holistic approach that integrates sustainability, health, and well-being, while transforming modes of production and consumption.

The Engines of the 6th Wave

The main drivers of this wave are:

- **Artificial Intelligence and Big Data** : AI continues to revolutionize industries, from finance to medicine to agriculture. Big Data enables unprecedented personalization of services and products.
- **Renewable Energy and Sustainability** : The transition to cleaner, more sustainable energy sources is becoming a global imperative, with innovations in energy storage, smart grids, and energy efficiency.

- **Biotechnology and Health** : Advances in biotechnology are enabling breakthroughs in personalized medicine, genetic engineering, and sustainable food production.
- **New Forms of Mobility and Urbanization** : Smart cities, autonomous vehicles, and sustainable infrastructure are redefining the way we live and interact with our environment.

Implications for the World Economy

This 6th wave of innovation promises to radically transform the global economy by making it more resilient, inclusive, and sustainable. However, it comes with challenges, including managing the transition for traditional industries, regulating new technologies, and adapting workforce skills.

Even if we manage to avoid a major correction caused by the AI bubble, the rise of the 6th wave will bring inevitable disruptions. These disruptions will require economic, regulatory, and social adjustments that could create market tensions, particularly when economic cycles like those of Juglar and Kondratieff reach their inflection point.

Sources :

- Visual Capitalist - The History of Innovation Cycles
- S&P Global Market Intelligence

Conclusion: Innovation Cycles and Bubbles, an Inevitable Balance of the Economy

The history of industrial revolutions and great waves of innovation teaches us a fundamental truth: each major technological transformation requires enormous investments and is accompanied by promises of growth which, inevitably, lead to the formation of speculative bubbles. Whether these bubbles burst or are resolved through corrections, this process is part of the natural balance of the global economy.

Bubbles, although feared, are often a symptom of radical innovation that profoundly changes the structure of industries. They represent a time of exuberance when capital flows to support future visions that, if realized, can transform the world. However, when expectations exceed economic realities, a correction becomes inevitable. This readjustment is necessary to make markets more healthy and realistic, thus making it possible to redefine the foundations of the next phase of growth.

Businessmen like **Warren Buffett** well illustrate the art of "riding the wave" during these periods of turbulence. Known for its disciplined investment strategy and counter-cyclical approach, Buffett's company, **Berkshire Hathaway**, has often taken advantage of financial crises to acquire undervalued assets. In 2008, for example, in the midst of the global financial crisis, Buffett invested heavily in companies like **Goldman Sachs** And **General Electric**, subsequently making substantial gains when markets recovered.

Other billionaires, such as **John Paulson** or **George Soros**, have also become famous for anticipating crises and taking advantage of market corrections to generate exceptional returns. Their success demonstrates that with rigorous analysis and a clear investment strategy, it is possible to transform periods of crisis into opportunities.

AI Bubble: How to Survive the Next Stock Market Crash

In conclusion, it is not a question of fearing bubbles and corrections, but of understanding that they are inevitable and part of the natural cycle of the economy. Preparing for them, knowing how to anticipate them, and being ready to act when opportunities present themselves, are the keys to not only surviving, but thriving in a constantly changing economic environment. As Warren Buffett says so well: "Be fearful when others are greedy, and greedy when others are fearful."

AI Bubble: How to Survive the Next Stock Market Crash

Annexes

Additional Resources for Investment

To deepen your knowledge and refine your investment strategies, here is a selection of useful resources:

- **Recommended Books** :
    - "*The intelligent investor*" by Benjamin Graham: An investing classic with an emphasis on value investing.
    - *"The Little Book of Stock Market Investing"* by John C. Bogle: A Practical Introduction to the Principles of Passive Investing.
    - *"Trading and AI: The New Era of Intelligent Investing"* : Guide to integrating artificial intelligence into investment strategies.
    https://amzn.eu/d/gratlko

    - "*The big illustrated book of economic cycles: Kondratiev, Schumpeter, Juglar, Kitchin*" for Thomas Andrieu : This book is a comprehensive reference on the major economic cycles that influence financial markets. It presents a detailed analysis of the cycle theories proposed by Kondratiev, Schumpeter, Juglar, and Kitchin, and offers clear illustrations to better understand the cyclical dynamics of the economy. It is an essential tool for investors looking to anticipate market reversals and adjust their strategies accordingly.
    https://amzn.eu/d/5U45FqH

    - *"Leveraged Trading"* par Romain Daubry
    Romain Daubry explores trading strategies using leverage. This book is aimed at traders looking to maximize their gains while effectively managing leverage risks. It is a must-have guide for those who want to deepen their trading techniques in a high volatility environment.

AI Bubble: How to Survive the Next Stock Market Crash

https://amzn.eu/d/fOZciU8

- **Websites, Platforms et newsletter** :
    - **Investopedia** : An online encyclopedia offering detailed explanations of financial concepts.
    - **Morningstar** : Analysis tools for mutual funds, stocks, and ETFs.
    - **TradingView** : Charting platform allowing you to follow the charts of stocks, cryptocurrencies, and other assets.
    - Tino Bernard Hugues' YouTube Channel: Tino Bernard Hugues regularly shares market analyses, trading advice, and investment strategies on his YouTube channel. His videos are accessible and well-researched, providing a great starting point for investors of all levels. Subscribe to his channel for regular updates: Tino Bernard Hugues - The Stock Exchange Podcast.
      https://www.youtube.com/channel/UCThl4vA0pKxcCu8TCv5T1hQ

    - **The Newsletter of *Nicolas Chéron*** : Nicolas Chéron, market strategist, offers a regular newsletter which offers detailed analyzes of financial markets, investment advice, and economic outlooks. This newsletter is a valuable resource for investors looking to stay informed about the latest market trends. You can subscribe to its newsletter via its official website: Nicolas Chéron - Official Website.
      https://nicolaskerous.fr

- **Online Courses** :
    - **Coursera - Finance** : Courses offered by renowned universities covering all aspects of finance and investment.
    - **Khan Academy - Finance and Investment** : Free and accessible courses for an introduction to basic financial concepts.

www.ingramcontent.com/pod-product-compliance
Lightning Source LLC
Chambersburg PA
CBHW052251220526
45471CB00001B/287